THE INDIAN RULING PRINCES AND THE NATIONAL MOVEMENT : 1927-47

The Indian Ruling Princes and the National Movement: 1927-47

SHIV KUMAR PRASAD SINGH

Commonwealth Publishers
NEW DELHI-110002
(INDIA)

Published by

COMMONWEALTH PUBLISHERS
4378/4B, GALI MURARI LAL
ANSARI ROAD, NEW DELHI-110002
INDIA

First Published, 1991

ISBN 81-7169-109-9

Printed at

Gaurav Printers
Maujpur
Delhi-110053

Dedicated
To
Late R.C.P. Sinha
My eldest brother to
whom I owe my entire
career.

Preface

With the emergence of Mahatma Gandhi on the political scene of India around 1920, the Indian nationalist movement became a mass movement, transcending all artificial divisions in the Indian sub-continent. The launching of the non-cooperation and civil disobedience movement removed the artificial barrier between British India and the princely states and broke down the isolation of the states from the rest of India. The British Government became more anxious to neutralise or at least to isolate the growing upsurge of Indian nationalism. This marked the beginning of the policy of utilising the services of the states for organising a counter-revolution.

The present work is a modest attempt to study the attitudes of the rulers and the people of princely states towards the national movement. It tries to analyse the role of the princes as imperial politicians and as a counter-weight against the nationalist movement. It also attempts to examine the origins and the growth of States People' movement in the wake of the non-cooperation and the civil disobedience movement. Besides, the relationship of the Indian National Congress with the States Peoples' movement and the All India States' Peoples' Conference is also dealt with. One of the chapters throws light on the federation plan as well as on the obstructionist policy of the princes which aimed at killing the federal plan comprising British India and the princely states. Such a pro-British attitude of the princes was visible during the second world war. While the Indian National Congress refused to co-operate with the British war efforts, the princes, on their part, reaffirmed their loyalty to the British crown and whole-heartedly supported the cause of the empire. The post-war developments affecting the states leading to the lapse of paramountcy and the integration of the states with the Indian union occupy a prominent place in this thesis.

The year 1927 was a landmark in the history of the Indian sub-continent : the States' Peoples' Movement was launched, ushering in an era of freedom struggle in the Indian States, in the modern political sense, which ended only with the end of the British raj in 1947.

Of late, several regional studies have been made on the political and social struggle of these states. These studies either treat the movement in isolation or make no distinction between the movement in the princely states and the movement in the neighbouring parts of British India. For example, R.L. Handa's *History of Freedom Struggle in Princely States* comes in the first category and that of N. Ramesham's, *The Freedom Struggle in Hyderabad* in the second. The first category does not take into consideration the interaction between the movement in British India and that in the states. Some other studies have equally failed by not taking into consideration the contradictions between the States Peoples' own ambitions and those of the British Indian nationalists. Besides, the general studies on the freedom movement of India hardly touches upon that segment of Indian population which lived in the princely states. The present study is an attempt to fill up this gap. It examines the interactions between the States Peoples' struggle against the autocratic regimes, with the British Indian nationalist struggle. The main features of the British policy towards these movements are also taken into account.

Apart from V.P. Menon's book there are useful published sources like the White Paper on the Indian States, various pamphlets and reports published by the All India States' Peoples' Conference, the proceedings of the Chamber of

Princes and the various official reports. The files of the Foreign and Political departments of the Indian government and the private papers of the contemporary stalwarts also provide valuable materials.

I am grateful to the Patna University for the award of Teacher-fellowship which I availed of for one and half years, enabling me to do the spade work for this study. I should like to thank the staff of Nehru Memorial Museum and Library, New Delhi, the National Archives, New Delhi, the Patna University Library, the Patna College Library, the Library of the Patna University History Department and the Sinha Library, Patna for their help and courtesy.

I take this opportunity to express my deep sense of gratitude to Dr. J.C. Jha, University Professor and formerly Head of the Department of History, Patna University, presently Director, Dr. K.P. Jayaswal Research Institute, Patna, for meticulously going through the study with the conscientiousness characteristic of him. I appreciate his help all the more, because it cost him many a precious moment of his busy time.

I must also record my grateful thanks to the late Dr. D.N. Verma, Professor of History, Patna University who, in fact, suggested this topic to me.

Words fail to express my indebtedness to my late father who allowed me to go to Delhi for research work even when he was almost on the deathbed.

I am deeply indebted to my elder brothers, the late Sri R.C.P. Sinha, A.D.M. Saharsa, and present Sri B P. Singh, I.A.S., Joint Secretary Mines, Government of India and Dr. R.P. Singh, Lecturer in Political Scienee, Bhagalpur University for inspiring and encouraging me from time to time. I thank my wife who helped me overcome many obstacles— personal and otherwise.

SHIV KUMAR PRASAD SINGH

Contents

1

Introduction

India is one geographical entity.[1] Yet throughout her long and chequered history both the centrifugal and the centripetal forces worked almost alternately. During the British rule, politically there were "two Indias, British India, governed by the crown according to the statutes of Parliament and enactments of the Indian Legislature, and the Indian States under the suzerainty of the crown and still for the most part under the personal rule of the Princes."[2] The Government of India Act defined the Indian States as including "any territory, whether described as a State, an Estate, a Jagir, or otherwise belonging to or under the suzerainty of His Majesty and not being a part of British India."[3] In political practice the term applied to a political community occupying a territory in India of defined boundaries and subject to a common ruler who enjoyed or exercised, as belonging to him, any of the functions and attributes of internal sovereignty duly recognised by the paramount power.[4]

---

1. उत्तरम् यत् समुद्रस्य हिमद्रिश्चैव दक्षिणम्
   वर्षं तद् भारतं नाम भारती यत्र सन्ततिः । विष्णु पुराण, II : 3 I.
2. *Butler Committee Report*, (opening paragraph), 1929.
3. *Government of India Act*, 1936, Sub-section (1) of Section 311.
4. *White Papers on Indian States*, Ministry of States, Government of India, Part II, p. 17.

The Butler Committee and the Simon Commission applied this elastic term to 562 units, whereas the Joint Parliamentary Committee of Indian Constitutional Reforms referred to 600 units as States. The term covered, at one end of the scale, units like Hyderabad and Kashmir which were of the size of the United Kingdom, and at the other end, minute holdings in Kathiawar extending only to a frew acres.[5]

Out of the total area enclosed within the territories of pre-partition India, i.e., 1,581,410 square miles, the Indian States covered an area of 715,964 square miles, which constituted about 45 per cent of the total Indian territories. In post-partition India, the area covered by the states geographically contiguous to the Dominion of India was reduced to 587,949 square miles, being about 48 per cent of the total area of the Dominion of India, viz., 1,221,072 square miles. The State of Kashmir with a territory of 82,332 square miles, constituted the largest territorial units amongst the states. There were 15 states which had territories of more than 10,000 square miles and 67 having territories ranging from 1,000 to 10,000 square miles. There were 202 states, each having an area of less than 10 square miles.[6]

The total population of the states according to the census figures of 1941 was 93.2 millions, constituting about 24 per cent of the total population of 389 millions of pre-partition India. After partition the total population of the Dominion of India was only 318.9 millions and of the states within the geographical orbit of Indian Dominion to 89 millions, changing the relative population ratio of the states from 24 per cent to 28 per cent.[7]

In pre-partition India 16 states had a population of over one million. These 16 states plus 4 others with a population

5. Ibid.
6. Ibid.
7. Ibid.

of more than 750,000 but less than a million were assigned individual representation in the Constituent Assembly of India. These 20 states claimed 60 per cent seats in the Constituent Assembly as against 33 per cent seats assigned to the rest of the states. Of these 20 states, 11 were entitled to send two or more representatives. Of the rest 13 had a population between 500,000 and 750,000. The remainders of the 140 states which were the members of the chamber of Princes in their own right, had a population ranging from 25,000 to 50,000.[8]

The distribution of the principal communities over the territories of the states in post-partition India showed that 27 per cent and 26 per cent respectively of the total population of the Hindus and the Muslims were to be found in the states. In the case of the Sikhs and the Indian Christians, however, the percentage was much higher : the states claimed 50 per cent of the Indian Christians 36 per cent of the Sikhs residing in the Dominion of India. The corresponding figures for pre-partition India were the Hindus 25 per cent, the Muslims 16 per cent, the Indian Christians 46 per cent and the Sikhs 27 per cent.[9]

The main feature that distinguished the states from the provinces of British India was that the former unlike the latter had not been annexed by the British. In their individual origin, however, the evolution and growth of the states represented different processes. First, there were the old established states, such as those in Rajputana which existed before the advent of the British rule. Another class consisted mainly of the states with Muslim dynasties which were founded by the nobles or the viceroys of the foreign invaders. Then there were the newer states, which the British recognised during the final stages of the consolidation of their power.[10]

The states were scattered all over the Indian sub-continent. The yellow and pink map of pre-partition India

---

8. Ibid.
9. Ibid.
10. Ibid., p. 19.

showed the Baluchistan states and the states of Kashmir and Sikkim on the frontiers of India. It showed the north-east Cooch-Bihar within the territories of the Bengal province and the Manipur state surrounded by the territories of the province of Assam. Down south the next bloc of Indian state territory was the chain of small states known as the Chhatisgarh and Orissa states. Further south figured the states of Hyderabad and Mysore. Facing the Indian ocean deepsouth were the two densely populated states of Cochin and Travancore. Northwards upto the west coast were the various Maratha states, the largest being Kolhapur. The chain of states ended with the State of Baroda made up of several separate areas to the north of the Bombay Presidency. To the north-west of Bombay lay a number of states the more important of which were Kutch, Nawanagar, Bhavnagar and Junagarh. To the north-east lay the Central Indian states which included Gwalior, Indore and Rewa. The northern and north-eastern portion of Bombay was separated from the Punjab by the wide area of Rajputana states. Important among these states were Bikaner, Jaipur, Jodhpur and Udaipur. The states of Punjab region were Patiala, Jind, Nabha and Kapurthala. In the United Province (now Uttar Pradesh) were to be found the isolated states of Tehri Garhwal, Rampur and Banaras.[11] The State of Khairpur lay in the geographical orbit of Sind.

Political Diversity of States : The internal administration of the states and their political set up varied greatly. There was a wide difference in the degree of administrative efficiency reached by the most advanced and the most backward. According to the information circulated by the Chamber of Princes in 1946, over 60 states had set up some form of legislative bodies.[12] In several others, schemes for associating the people with the governance of their states were under consideration. In most cases, the development of representative institutions did not approximate to the growth of self-governing institutions in the provinces, which were on the

---

11. Ibid.
12. *Report of the Chamber of Princes*, 1946, p. 16.

threshold of complete freedom. However, everywhere there was a growing consciousness of the rights and liberties of the people and a new spirit was abroad.

Three Categories of States : According to the Butler Committee the Indian States as they existed could be classified into three distinct categories : (i) The states, the rulers of which were the members of the Chamber of Princes in their own right, were 108 in number. (ii) The number of the states whose rulers were represented in the Chamber of Princes by twelve members of their order elected by themselves, was 127. (iii) The estates, jagirs and others, 327 in number.[13]

The first category included the ruling princes who enjoyed a permanent dynastic salute of 11 guns or more, together with other rulers of the states who exercised such full or practically full internal powers as, in the opinion of the viceroy qualified them for individual admission to the chamber. As a result of fresh admissions, the membership of the chamber was enlarged to 140.

Nature of Paramountcy : The sovereignty over the states was divided between the British Government and the rulers of the states in proportions which differed greatly according to the history and importance of the several states, and which were regulated by the treaties, engagements, *sanads* and the usage. The territories of British India and of the Indian states were inextricably interlaced. The territories of the Indian states were intersected by British railway lines, postal lines and telegraph lines. Though the points of contact between British India and the princely states were many, the latter were slow in assimilating the new principles and ideals, methods and practices current in the former.[14] Over a century the states had dotted the political map of India as disruptive patches retarding the political and economic integration of the life of the people.[15] Taken together, the states constituted a

---

13. Ibid., p. 17.
14. S.R. Mehrotra, *Towards India's Freedom and Partition*, p. 241.
15. *White Paper on Indian States*, p. 133.

great cruciform barrier, broken by gaps of varying width, but more or less effectively separating the different parts of British India from one another. This fact has obvious strategic and political importance. New forces of contitutional development and national movement were beginning to pose problems which could not be solved by keeping India divided into two watertight compartments. It was an artificial division artificially maintained. But even with the best will in the world, the marriage of Indian India with British India would not have been an easy task as the British surely were not eager to act as the priest. In fact, they had a vested interest in perpetuating the division.[16]

The Revolt of 1857 demonstrated the value of the 'yellow patches' to the British Government. Except for minor defections, the Indian Princes not only remained aloof from the rising but, in certain cases, extended effective assistance to the British to suppress it. No wonder Canning, the Governor-General of India, gratefully acknowledged the role of the states as the "breakwaters in the storm which would have swept over in one great wave."[17] It was now realized that the states could play a most helpful rule as a bulwark against the forces of nationalism. This led to a radical change in the British policy towards the states. The new policy found expression in 1858. Queen Victoria's proclamation promised, "We shall respect the rights, dignity and honour of native Princes as our own and there would be no further conquests." In 1861 the *sanads* were issued which guaranteed the princes, big and small, their status and acknowledged their right of adoption. The *sanads* were intended to remove mistrust and suspicion and to "reassure and knit the native sovereigns to paramount power."[18] No more was heard of annexation as the only means of granting the "blessings" of civilized government to the "suffering millions." Under the new system

---

16. S.R. Mehrotra, op. cit., p. 241.
17. V.P. Menon, *The Story of the Integration of the Indian States* (first published in 1956), p. 9.
18. Ibid.

described as that of 'subordinate union', the supreme power accepted its moral responsibility for a minimum of good government, security, law and order within the territories of the Indian states. The system basically differed but little from the earlier system of subordinate isolation. However, the policy of cutting the knot which the prevailing practice had failed to untie so vigorously pursued by Dalhousie[19] now gave way to a policy of more window-dressing.[20]

The new policy aimed at consolidating not the territories but the powers of the British Government. Paramountcy of the British crown was the coping-stone of the imperial edifice in India. It constituted at once a link and a barrier. It provided a nexus between British India and states and thereby integrated the economic and administrative life of the country. At the same time it drove a wedge between the two parts of India. The policy of 'Hands off the Indian States' in British India with its reciprocal implication of 'Hands off British Indian concern' for states, which reared up high walls of isolationism around the states could be made effective only by the operation of the paramountcy.[21]

Until the last phase of the first world war (1912-18) Indian nationalism had not developed into a real challenge to the foreign rule in India. This great war greatly affected the temper of Indian nationalism.

With the appearance of Mohandas Karamchand Gandhi[22] on the political stage and the introduction of the Montagu-Chelmsford reforms,[23] the nationalist movement fired

---

19. The Governor-General of India, 1848-56.
20. *White Paper on Indian States*, p. 12.
21 Ibid. p. 13.
22. Born 1869; died 1948. See Bimal Prasad, *Gandhi, Nehru and J.P. : Studies in Leadership*, Chanakya Publications, Delhi, 1984, pp. 1-85.
23. Ibid., p. 5 : This report failed to satisfy India's nationalist leadership.

the imagination of the people and deepened the anxiety of the British rulers of India to neutralise, or at least to isolate the growing upsurge of Indian nationalism by using the princes as a counterweight. This marked the beginning of the policy of utilising the services of the states for organising a counter revolution.[24]

Under the smokescreen of bringing together Indian India and British India the British organised a chamber of Princes on 8 February 1921 which did little more than promoting a joint action on the part of the Indian states and bringing them closer to the political department of the Government of India.[25]

The formation of this new body had other important consequences. So far the Indian questions had been a triangular one involving the British, the Indian nationalists and the Muslim communalists. From now onwards another dimension was introduced into the conflict and with the involvement of the Indian states it became quadrangular. It was this quadrangular situation which we encounter at the Round Table conference in the early 1930s and in the Government of India Act of 1935.[26]

The establishment of the chamber did not affect the individual relations between any state and the crown, but it involved a deviation from the earlier policy under which the crown discouraged joint action and deliberation between the Indian states.[27]

The relationship of the states with the Government of India had now to be reviewed in the light of the possible constitutional developments in British India. It was thought that the growing administrative unity between the states and

---

24. White Paper, op. cit. p. 15.
25. S.R. Mehrotra, op. cit., p. 241.
26. Ibid.
27. *White Paper on Indian States*, p. 21.

the rest of India would detract from their role as breakwaters. Therefore an attempt was now made "to convert the Indian states into an Indian ulster by pressing constitutional theories into service."[28] It was in this context that the theory of the crown as the sole link between the central government and the states was systematically developed.[29]

The Butler Committee appointed in 1927 to report on the grievances of the princes and on the nature of paramountcy while summarily turning down the request of the princes for a definition of the scope of paramountcy and the codification of the political practice, readily agreed with the Council of States that "the relationship of the states to the paramount power is a relationship to the crown.[30] Of all the demands made by the princes, the Butler Committee clearly and forcefully recognised only one, that for making any transfer of the crown's rights and obligations in relation to the states to the persons not under the crown's authority, conditional on the agreement of the states. In paragraph 58 of the Report of the Committee said, "The States demand that without their own agreement the rights and obligations of the paramount power should not be assigned to persons who are not under its control, for instance an Indian Government in British India responsible to an Indian Legislature. If any Government in the nature of a dominion government should be constituted in British India, such a government would clearly be a new government resting on a new and written constitution." True, such a contingency had not arisen. However, they were bound "to draw attention to the really grave apprehension of the princes on this score and to record our strong opinion that in view of the fact of the historical nature of the relationship between paramount power and the Princes, the latter should not be transferred without their own agreement to a relationship with a new government in British India responsible to an India Legislature."[31]

28. Ibid p. 15.
29. Ibid.
30. *Butler Committee Report*, 1929, para 56.
31. Ibid.

The new concept of personal relationship between the states and the crown found expression in the Act of 1935 and drove further the wedge between the states and the rest of India. Paramountcy which become "the method by which the executive of British India aggrandised itself at the expense of the Indian states" now set in motion the reverse process of depriving the British Indian Executive of all constitutional status vis-a-vis the states."[32] In complete regard of patent historical facts and the established constitutional procedure a new functionary, the crown's representative, was now brought into existence to conduct the relations of the crown with the states. The relations between the states and the Government of India were hereafter to be through the circuitous route of the crown's representative. At one stroke of the pen, the states were thus delinked from the Governor-General-in-Council and 'pegged' to the British crown. The policy of balance and counterpoise thus forged for the imperial political armoury another formidable weapon, the problem of the states.[33]

The theory of 'personal contract' or 'personal obligations' illustreates the opportunistic approach to the whole question of the status of the Indian states. The increasing emphasis on the crown as the paramount power in relation to the states and the interposition of the crown representative between the Government of India and the states, were constitutional innovytions calculated to deprive the successor government at the centre of its legitimate status vis-a-vis the states and to impede the evolution of an organic political and fiscal relationship between the centre and the states.[34]

The theory of personal contract disregarded not only historical facts but also the usage and sufferance which had come to be recognised as the principal factors governing the relationship between the states and the paramount power.[35]

---

32. *White Paper on Indian States*, p. 16.
33. Ibid.
34. Ibid.
35. Ibid.

The committee appointed by the All-India Parties Conference in 1928, under the chairmanship of Motilal Nehru to draft a constitution for India, examining the theory of 'personal contract' which was first openly advocated on behalf of some of the princes by this counsel in a letter to *The Law Quarterly Review*, expressed itself as follows : "The Princes in making these contracts gave their confidence to the British crown and nation and the crown cannot assign the contracts to any third party, The British Government as paramount power has undertaken the defence of all the States, and, therefore, to remain in India with whatever military and naval forces may be requisite to enable it to discharge that obligation. It cannot hand over these forces to any other government—to a foreign power such as France, or Japan, to a dominion government such as Canada or Australia; nor even to British India."[36]

Thus an effective barrier was put up against the progress of British India towards Dominion status. The British nation must always maintain adequate military and naval forces to discharge its obligations to the Indian states.

Dealing with the contention that the British Government could not transfer their treaty obligations to any other power or even to British India, the committee argued that this ignored "the settled practice of the Government of India and, by invoking so-called first principles in determining the legal relationships, it overlooks the hard and unchallengeable fact that from the early days of the Company it has been the Government of India and the Government of India alone which has dealt with Indian Princes and Indian States."[37] It asserted that this introduced an element of 'personal confidence' between them and the British nation which was difficult to understand : "It suggests that the past and present Government of India

---

36. *The Law Quarterly Review*, 1927, p. 28.
37. *All Parties Conference*, 1928, *Report of the Committee and Summary of Proceedings* (Allahabad, All India Congress Committee, 1928), p. 13.

which have so far exercised the power, said to be degenerated from the crown, were and are acceptable to the Indian Princes and Indian States; but that the future government of India, if it is to be dominion type, will not be acceptable. This in plain English means the past and present Governments of India were acceptable because they were essentially foreign in their composition and not responsible to the Indian electorate and that future Government of India would not be acceptable to the Indian Princes because it will consist of their own countrymen and because it will be responsible to an electorate of their own countrymen."[38]

The theory that the head of a state could, in his personal capacity, enter into treaty engagements having far reaching effect on the destinies of the people, is too anachronistic to be maintained in the twentieth century. However, the theory came to stay; it further widened the cleavage between the princes and the people and drove the princes deeper into the imperial fold.[39]

The new concept encouraged separatist tendencies and obstructionist tactics in the princely quarters. Coupland, comparing the attitude of the princes with that of the Muslim League, observed that they would insist quite as firmly on disrupting India "rather than accept an all-India system of government which over-rode their rights and put them at the mercy of the conquerors and the High Command." "Nor would it be", he went on to say, "reasonable on the British Government's part to rule that out." Fed on such theories, the princes naturally subscribed even so late as the eve of the Cripps Mission (1942) to the policy embodied in the following resolution unanimously adopted by the chamber of princes: "That this chamber has repeatedly made it clear that any scheme to be acceptable to the states must effectively protect their rights arising from the Treaties, Engagements and Sanads or otherwise and ensure the future existence, sovereignty and

38. *White Paper on Indian States*, p. 140.
39. Ibid.

autonomy of the states thereunder guaranteed and leave them complete freedom duly to discharge the obligations to the crown and to their subjects; it therefore notes with particular satisfaction the reference in the announcement of the Prime Minister to the fulfilment of the Treaty obligations to the Indian States."[40]

It would be wrong to assume that this resolution really represented the unanimous wishes of the princes, it was only an indication of the complex which rendered it impossible for the princes to think of India freed from the foreign yoke, or of a constitutional relationship with the government at the centre in which the crown did not find a place.

This change of policy both on the part of the British Government and the princely rulers led the latter to act as political allies of their British patron. The change was also responsible for the beginning of the princely involvement in the political events in the sub-continent when the British Indian politicians seriously challenged the British Raj.[41] Within their own territories the princes had reasonably firm control over the situation through their paternalist activities and their employment of autocratic methods against the sources of opposition. When they entered the political arena of British India, the princes carried not only their subjects but also their attitudes shaped by the methods they utilized and the security they enjoyed within their states. They therefore possessed both assets and liabilitis for dealing with the Indian politicians who earnestly wanted to be treated honourably and set before themselves the goal of responsible governments.[42]

The authors of the Montagu-Chelmsford Report (1918) noted, "There is a strong reason why the present stir in British India cannot be a matter of indifference to the princes. Hopes

---

40. *Resolution of the Chamber of Princes*, 1942.
41. Barbara N. Ramusack, 'The Civil Disobedience Movement and the Round Table Conferences : The Princes Response', B.R. Nanda (ed.), *The Essays on Modern Indian History*, p 107.
42. Ibid.

and aspirations may overlap frontier lines like sparks across a street. There are in the Native States men of like minds to those who have been active in spreading new ideas in India. It is not our task to prophesy, but no one would be surprised if constitutional change in British India quickened the pace in the Native States as well."[43]

During the eleven years following this prophesy immense change took place in India. Hopes and aspirations overleft the frontiers long ago and the sparks had already kindled the fire. While a large majority of the people of states were demanding responsible government, a section was growing demanding a complete wiping out of the princes, just as the cry for complete severance of British connection was fast gaining ground in British India.[44]

The Maharajas apprehended that the advancing tide of democracy in British India would sweep them away. They began to talk of treaties made a century ago in circumstances entirely different from those that existed in the 1920s. Dealing with this talk of treaties Srinivas Sastri[45] said in his Cochin address, "when everything else changes, when the British crown is going to be replaced as far as the final control of Indian affairs is concerned by the Indian People, when the tremendous revolution is going to take place are these treaties the last word of human progress, even where India is concerned?"[46]

They were ruthlessly suppressing the exposition of public opinion. Not a day passed without hearing the news of some Maharaja or another issuing *letters de catchet* to prohibit

---

43. *Montagu-Chelmsford Report*, Para 157.
44. P.L. Chudgar, *Indian Princes under British Protection*, p. 159.
45. Sastri (1869-1946) attended the League of Nations as an Indian delegate in 1921 and in 1922 attended the Limitation of Naval Armaments Conference in Washington as the head of the Indian delegation. See S.P. Sen (ed.), *Dictionary of National Biography*, Calcutta, 1974, Vol. IV, p. 175.
46. Chudgar, op. cit., p. 157.

public meetings, summarily arresting and imprisoning public and respectable citizens, wholesale arbitrary confiscation of property and banishment of people from their native land.[47]

The people had long tolerated the arbitrary rule of the princes and its dire consequences. Under its dead weight their soul was almost killed, but now there began a new stirring of life. They began to organise themselves and their organisations began to gather momentum as the numerous conferences of the people of the various states show.

The gradual strengthening of the national movement had its impact on the political structure of British India. Gradually, representative institutions of a parliamentary character with the rudiments of a responsible government began to emerge in the provinces under the Dyarchy. In the Indian states, however, with the popular movements yet to acquire any measure of power, the political set-up continued to be autocratic wherein democratic institutions even in an elementary form did not exist.[48] With the exception of certain states like Travancore, Cochin, Mysore and Porbandar, most of the states were autocracies. Whether it was a big state like Hyderabad,[49]

---

47. Ibid.
48. Urmila Phadnawis, *Towards the Integration of Indian States*, 1919-1947, p. 80.
49. Discussing the abject conditions of the people, a Hyderabadi wrote, "The Government had turned a deaf ear to the representation of the people persistently made during the last decades or so far (a) expansion of the legislature; (b) reform in the educational policy of Government; (c) improvement in the system of recruitment and morale of services; (d) impartiality in the granting of concessions." A citizen, pseud, *Under the Rule of His Exalted Highness—Conditions in Nizam State* (Poona, Vaidic Ashram, 1938).

    The state was in fact ruled by *firmans* issued at any time in accordance with the whim and caprice of the ruler. The people did not enjoy civil liberty. D.R. Rao (ed.), *Misrule of Nizam*, being extracts from and translation of articles on Mir Osman Ali Bahadur, the Nizam of Hyderabad (Madras, Suryakant Press, 1926), pp. 24-25.

Kashmir[50] or Patiala[51] or one of the smaller states of Orissa[52] or central India,[53] or the Himalayan States,[54] popular representatives had no say whatsoever in the affairs of the states. In fact, in the case of these smaller states, "the rulers' autocratic power was still tempered only by the use and wont, or, as in many Maratha states by the rights of a feudal landed aristocracy."[55]

The Indian freedom struggle which had assumed a national dimension with the establishment of the Indian National Congress in 1885, entered a new phase of non-cooperation with the British government in 1920 when Gandhi became its supreme leader and a new phase of non-violent struggle for freedom began.[56] Some of the nationalist leaders often took refuge in the states and continued their activities from there. This was the first contact the states' people had with the nationalist movement.[57]

The participation of the troops of the Indian rulers in the first world war brought them into contact with the outside

---

50. P.N. Bazaz, *History of Struggle for Freedom in Kashmir* (Delhi, Kashmir Publishing Co., 1954), pp. 140-41. Prem Nath Bazaz (born 1905) started his political career in 1930. Following Mahatma Gandhi's path of non-violence to secure for Kashmir responsible government. Brought out a paper *Hamdard* to propogate nationalism, secularism and democracy. He was arrested for six months in 1938 See S.P. Sen, op. cit., Vol. I, p. 148.
51. *All india States' Peoples' Conference, Indictment of Patiala, Report* Bombay AISPC, 1930, pp. 1-37.
52. *All India States' Peoples' Conference, Orissa States' Enquiry Report*, Bombay AISPC, 1939, pp. 1-39.
53. Kachru, D.N., *The Jhabna Tragedy*, Bombay, AISPC, n.d., pp. 1t 26.
54. *Himalaya States' Peoples' Conference, Proceedings and Resolutions*, April, 1938, pp. 1-6.
55. R. Coupland, *Indian Politics*, 1936-42, Oxford University Press, Lodon, 1944, pp. 167-8.
56. B.N. Pandey, *The Break-up of British India*, Macmillan, London, 1969, pp. 110-13.
57. Urmila Phadnavis, *Towards the Integration of Indian States* (Based on a discussion with Mr. Jaynarain Vyas, M.P.), p. 84.

world, making them familiar with the rights of self-government. In 1917 the British Government announced its 'August Declaration', promising the right of self-determination to the Indian people. No sooner had these returned soldiers made their own people in the states familiar with such ideas and promises Mahatma Gandhi gave a clarion call for mass support to the national movement. This had its impact on the people of the states also.[58] Hitherto supine and complacent, they now began to feel restive. Local organisations were organised and the Indian National Congress, on its part began to take note of these developments. On the top of that some political organisations in the states for the first time called upon the princes to grant, at once, full responsible government in the states.[59] It, however, made it clear in 1927 that while the states' People could become the member of the Congress, they could not organisationally interfere with the internal affairs of the states.[60]

Meanwhile, some of the leading political workers concerned with the problems of the states took the initiative and decided to found a central organisation to provide a leadership to the movements in the states. The immediate impulse for the founding of this organisation appears to have been the appointment of the Indian States' Committee under the chairmanship of Harcourt Butler on 16 December 1927. Soon after the announcement of the Committee, the leading workers in the cause of the states' people like Balwantray Mehta,[61]

58. Ibid.
59. For example, the Kathiawar Political Conference, the Baroda Praja Mandal, the Deccan States' Conference, Mysore States Congress, Indore Praja Mandal, Idar Praja Mandal, Hyderabad States' Peoples' Conference, and Jamnagar and Nawanagar Praja Mandals.
60. *Indian National Congress 1920-23*, Law Journal Press, Allahabad (date not clear) no. 36.
61. Mehta (1899-1965) joined the non-cooperation movement in 1920 and fought for the democratisation of the administration of Bhavnagar and other princely states in Saurashtra. In 1921 he worked for the Kathiawad Political Conference and in 1923 helped the foundation of the Bhavnagar Praja Mandal : S.P. Sen (ed), op. cit. Vol. III, p. 70.

Manilal Kothari and G.R. Abhayankar convened the All India States' People's Conference in December 1927.

The second phase of the non-cooperation movement produced a deep impact on the minds of the people of these states and stirred them into political activity. Popular struggles were waged in many states, particularly in Rajkot, Jaipur. Kashmir, Hyderabad and Travancore. The National Congress supported the states' Peoples' Movement and urged the princes to introduce democratic representative government and to grant fundamental civil rights to the people. The States Peoples' movement thus brought about an unprecedented national consciousness among the people of the states. It also awakened a sense of national unity all over India.[62]

Karen Leonard, in a recent article[63] says that the Indian nationalist movement was not meaningfully mounted in any princely state. According to him, the nationalist movements, in the usual sence of some degree of mass mobilization of the people rallying to a modern nation state, were rare in the princely states of India.[64] Only by retreating from the requirement of mass-mobilization, and allowing nationalism focussed on a princely state rather than on the future nation-state envisaged by the Indian National Congress, can we find examples of nationalist movements.[65] Undoubtedly, there were social, cultural and political movements of various types in the princely states. Trying to discuss them under the rubric of the nationalist movement in the princely states is like trying to dissuss the 1857 Mutiny or rebellion as war of independence.[66] There was not one movement; there were

62. *Indian National Congress, 1920-23*, op. cit. p. 43. Also see *Indian National Congress* (*Resolutions*) 1927, N.28, 49 and Bipan Chandra, *Modern India*, p. 296.
63. Karan Leonard, 'Aspects of Nationalist Movement in the Princely States of India', *The Quarterly Review of Historical Studies*, Vol. XXI, 1981-82, no. 2 and 3, p. 3.
64. Ibid.
65. Ibid.
66. Ibid.

many; there were political issues and casts of characters specific to one religion or state, and there were interconnections between the All India States' Peoples' Conference and Mahatma Ghandhi who had "some centrality, who lent some degree of meaning or method to the diverse activities" under review.[67]

Those who look hard for nationalist activities in the princely states often explain their lack of success by applying a sweeping generalization about the nationalist movement in British India to the princely states; that the nationalist mobilization reflected the rate of social change, and that the states were "backward". The assumption is that where processes like western education, urbanization, and industrialization had proceeded furthest, the population was most involved in the political movement for a modern nation state. Anil Seal[68] sets forth a wealth of quantitative evidence, trying to relate the progress of western education—the numbers of graduates at different levels, their employment pattern—to the political activities in the British Indian provinces. Extending this reasoning to the princely states, one could compare the states with each other and with British India on measures of social change. But the range is very wide indeed, and there are examples where political activity more than nationalist activity does not correlates exactly with the rates of educational progress or urbanization. One may think of Baroda, Cochin and Travancore for their high rates of literacy and education, but these states evinced little political mobilization or nationalist or other issues. Mewar, on the other hand, though little modernized, presented the scenario of well-organised peasant agitations in the 1920s.[69]

An attempt to correlate measures of social change with political activity produces problems. Robin Jefferey, the

---

67. Ibid.
68. Anil Seal, *The Emergence of Indian Nationalism*, Cambridge, 1968, p. 38.
69. R. Ray, *Mewar : The Breakdown of the Princely Order*, pp. 205-239.

editor of a recent book on princely states, emphasizes urbanization in his discussion of the urban-based 1938 agitations for the responsible government which occurred in may states.[70] The hypothesis is "as difficult to disprove as to prove." That kind of historical anthropology has not been done in either British or Princely India.[71]

Rather than compare the major princely states on measures of social change and devise reasons for their failure to explain political trends, the two real characteristics of the princely states must be differentiated from British India which had clear implications for the development of political movements in the states. Any discussion of these characteristics should clarify the issue of "backwardness" and give us another way of looking at political or nationalist activities in the princely states.

The first characteristic shared by the most important princely states in the 20th century was the reliance upon a modern administrative elite drawn from British India.[72] The princely states thus passed from the patrimonial systems of government to modern bureaucratic systems.[73] This western educated 'foreign' administrative elite was frequently supported by the British resident. Different sets of outside administrators like the Muslims from Delhi and the Brahmanas from Madras were imported by the states. The social and political configurations differed greatly, but almost all of the princely states followed this pattern. Jeffrey states that of the important, developed states only Baroda avoided the use of outsiders for bureaucratic modernization.[74]

---

70. Robin Jefferey, (ed.), *People, Princes and Paramount Power*, Delhi, 1978, pp. 13-14.
71. Karen Leonard, op. cit. p. 3.
72. Barbara N. Ramusack, *The Princes of India in the Twilight of Empire* (Columbus 1978), p. 109.
73. Mexweber, *The Theory of Social and Economic Organisation*, T. Parsons ed. (New York, 1964) pp. 346-58,
74. R, Jeffrey, *People, Princes and Paramount Power*, p. 22. However, Aurobindo Ghosh did serve the Baroda state first in the revenue department and then as a professor.

All important positions were monopolized by the outsiders in the Hyderabad State and in some other states. Even in Patiala, the Sikh State noted for administrative efficiency, the Prime Ministers in the 20th century were outsiders, and the first Sikh Prime Minister was appointed only in the 1940s.[75] It had become harder for the local men to enter the modern administration.[76] As local men gained western education in the states, they wanted their entry into the administration by displacing the 'foreign' British Indian elites.

The second characteristic shared by most of the princely states was an interest in the administrative but not political modernization. The modernizing officials confined their goals to the efficient performance of minimal government functions; the collection of taxes and the maintenance of law and order. Even in the most developed states, political modernization was conceived of as quite distinct from administrative modernization and was simply ignored. Nothing like representative institutions were sougth to be established.

With these two characteristics in mind one can comprehend the political agitations which occurred in many princely states since 1927. The States' Peoples' Movement became an integral part of the all-India Nationalist Movement.[77]

This book aims at studying the role of the princely states in the Indian national movement, pinpointing three aspects :

(a) the use by the British of the Indian States as a conservative bloc against the Indian Nationalist Movement;

---

75. Ibid.
76. K. Leonard, *Hyderabad : The Multi-non-Muli Conflict*, pp. 65-106. Also, E Haynes *Alwar : Bureaucracy versus Traditional Rulership*, pp. 32-64.
77. J. Wood, "Rajkot : Indian Nationalism in the Princely Context" in Jeffrey (ed.), *People, Princes and Paramountcy*, p. 240.

(b) the hostile attitude of some of the princes to the nationalist struggle in order to retain their independent identity; and

(c) the States' Peoples' Movement directed both against the autocratic princely rule and the British paramountcy. Indeed, in order to counter the Indian Nationalist Movement the British played two trump cards, one, the Muslims; and the other, the states. In the long run, the first proved to be a success; but the second proved to be a failure.[78] The relative failure of the British in using the states against the Indian struggle for freedom and unity was due to many factors :

(i) the lack of unity among the Indian States,

(ii) the lack of support from the subjects of the Indian princes;

(iii) the dissatisfaction of the Indian princes with the Government of India's Political Department; and

(iv) the patriotism of some of the Indian princes.[79]

---

78. S.R. Mehrotra, op. cit, p. 241.
79. Ibid.

2

The Rise of the States' Peoples' Movement

The year 1927 was a turning point in the history of the princely states as it witnessed the birth of a revolutionary upsurge under the banner of the All India States' Peoples' Conference with headquarters in Bombay. It was one of the major developments because the activities of the All India States Conference carried and spread the national movement to the princely states.[1] The princely states were the most formidable and oppressive stronghold of feudalism.[2] Appalling economic, political and social conditions prevailed in most of them. Peasants were oppressed, land revenue and taxation were excessive and unbearable, education was retarded, health and other social services were extremely backward, and freedom of the press and other civil rights hardly existed. The bulk of the state revenues were spent on the luxuries of the prices. In several states serfdom, slavery and forced labour were practised. In the pre-British days a corrupt and decadent ruler was checked to some extent by the challenge of internal revolt or external aggression. The British

---

1. Bipan Chandra, *Modern India* p. 295.
2. Sumit Sarkar, *Modern India*, p. 341.

rule freed the princes of both these dangers, and they felt free to indulge in gross misgovernment.[3]

Naturallyenough, many grievances existed and the growing wave of nationalist mass movement began to sweep the states' peoples too. There arose some pressure groups demanding political and social reforms in the princely states. During the years after the first world war, some British Indian politicians began to think that British India could never achieve self-government unless the states shared in democratic political advances.[4] Joined by a small but militant number of subjects of the states, these British Indian activists formed local groups. In the beginning these groups were regionally oriented but gradually they formed the All India States' Peoples' Conference to co-ordinate them.

The All India States' Peoples' Conference was, however, a very moderate body, confined to drawing up petitions and issuing pamphlets for representative institutions.[5] Some of their manifestoes even contained expressions of sympathy and support for the princes in their efforts to maintain their rights and status vis-a-vis the paramount power.[6] The first national meeting of the All India States' Peoples' Conference, held in December 1927, called for a federal arrangement between the two parts of India, an amalgamation of smaller states into politically and economically viable units, political reforms such as an independent judiciary and responsible ministers within the states' governments and various social and educational reforms.[7] The conference urged that "for a speedy

---

3. Bipan Chandra, op. cit., 295.
4. Barbara N. Ramusack, 'The Civil Disobedience Movement and the Round Table Conference', op. cit , p. 110.
5. *Tribune*, 1 June 1922, p.1; Mitra, *Indian Quarterly Register* II, July-December, 1924, pp. 494-8 and July-December 1925, 374-5.
6. Ibid, July-December, 1924, pp. 495-6.
7. AISPC, *Report of the Bombay Session*, 17 and 18 December 1978, Bombay, 1978. Also see *V.S. Srinivas Sastri : A Political Biography*, Bombay, 1963, pp. 201-5.

attainment of Swarajya, as a whole, the Indian States should be brought into constitutional relations with British India and the people of Indian States should be assigned a definite place and an effective voice in all matters of common concern in any new constitution that may be devised for the whole of India."[8] The conference thus explained its stand on the constitutional problems of the states from the point of view of the states' people and decided to place them before the Indian States' Committee.

The All-India States' Peoples' Conference, at the outset, was faced with a handicap. The Indian States' committee refused to recognise its claim to represent the states' people on the plea that legally and politically, only the princes were entitled to represent the people. The committee even refused to give the All-India States' Peoples' Conference its questionnaire. The All-India States' Peoples' Conference asserted that it represented the organization of the states' people and therefore it was fully entitled to express its views before the states committee. Finally, however, after a great deal of correspondence, the Indian States Committee agreed to receive a memorandum in which the conference could express its views on all matters within the terms of reference of the committee.[9]

While the memorandum was being prepared, the Executive Committee of the Conference appointed a delegation to be deputed to England to create public opinion abroad in support of the states' people. The delegation consisted of Dewan Bahadur Ramchandra Rao, G.R. Abhayankar, Amritlal D. Sheth and Sri P.L. Chudgar.

In spite of these efforts of the conference, not much attention was paid to its proposals. The Butler Committee

---

8. A.N. Sundarisanon, *Indian States Register and Directory*, Madras, Indian States' Registry Office, 1929, pp. 303-5.
9. *AISPC Memorandum of the Indian States' People*, Part III, Bombay, AISPC, 1929, p. 11.

presented no proposal for the political advancement of the states' people.[10]

This resulted in the denunciation of the Butler Report by the conference. Discussing it in the second session, its president, C.Y. Chintamani, said that " the Butler Committee was bad in its origin, bad in its time chosen for its appointment, bad in its terms of reference, bad in its personnel, bad in its line of enquiry."[11] In the meantime, the states' people found encouragement from the leading nationalists of British India. The All Parties Conference, in its report on the Dominion Constitution of India, laid down in clear terms that it visualised a representative form of government in the states in the event of a federal constitution being accepted by them. The All-India States' Peoples' Conference also obtained the support of some of the Congress leaders in the Calcutta Session of 1928 and the Lahore Session of 1929 of the Indian National Congress. In his presidential address at the Lahore Session, Jawaharlal Nehru said, "The Indian States cannot live apart from the rest of India and their rulers must, unless they accept their inevitable limitations, go the way of others who thought like them. And the only people who have the right to determine the future of the states must be the people of these states."[12] The Calcutta Session as well as the Lahore Session of the Congress adopted resolutions urging the princes to introduce "responsible government based on representative institutions in the states", and assuring the states' people its sympathy and support in their "legitimate and peaceful struggle" for the attainment of responsible government.[13]

---

10. *Foreign and Political Department*, no. 62, Special, 1931.
11. C.Y. Chintamani, *Presidental Address*, 1929. Chintamani (1880-1941) was a Great journalist who edited *The Leader* of Allahabad. He was the General Secretary of National Liberal Federation of India (1918-20 and 1923-29). He attended the first Round Table Conference in London.
12. *Report of the Forty-fourth Session of the Indian National Congress*, Lahore, AICC, 1929, p. 75.
13. *IΛC. RES*, 1928, no. 28, p. 33.
    INC. RES, 1927, no. 28, p. 57.

Though the Congress did not adopt any resolution on the states in its Karachi Session (1928), Mahatma Gandhi had, even earlier, in one of his speeches, maintained that the Congress represented the whole of India and wished that the rulers of the states would not take an uncompromising attitude. He maintained that "an undiluted autocracy, however, benevolent it may be, and an undiluted democracy are an incompatible mixture bound to result in an explosion." Mahatma Gandhi, however, in his characteristic way maintained that the Congress should not interfere with the internal affairs of the states and hoped that the princes could be prevailed upon to improve their administration.

Gandhi's views created doubts in the minds of some of the leaders of the states' people and N.C. Kelkar,[14] the President of the conference, sought clarification from Gandhi. In the correspondence that ensued, Mahatma Gandhi maintained that the policy of non-interference in the states was both "wise and sound."[15] The states under British law, he said, were independent entities and the Congress, therefore, could not interfere in their internal affairs. Gandhi believed, however, that in any event, a movement started from without could not be successful and wanted the people of the states to stand on their own feet.[16]

While in the earlier period there were few, who questioned the Congress stand, it did not go unchallenged during 1933-35. A radical group inside the Congress, which had constituted itself in 1934 into the Congress Socialist Party demanded that the Congress should take a more positive attitude towards the states. The Party held that the system

---

14. Narasimha Chintaman Kelkar (1872-1947) went to England in 1918 as the Secretary to the Home Rule League deputation to Parliament, was elected to the Indian Legislature on the Swaraj ticket in 1923, presided over the Hindu Mahasabha sessions of 1927 and 1929 and presided over the Marathi Literary Conferences in 1922 and 1930.
15. M.K. Gandhi, *Indian States, Problem*, p. 64.
16. Ibid., p. 65.

of monarchy, even if it was a constitutional one, was unsuitable for the states and called for a radical transformation of the political system of the states. The Congress Socialist Party, however, does not appear to have[17] been very effective in influencing the Congress, for, in 1935 the Congress Working Committee passed a detailed resolution restating its policy of non-interference. Evidently, to satisfy the All-India State's peoples' Conference and the leftist opinion, the Congres-maintainned that it would not sacrifice their interests to "buy the support of princes", for the implementation of the federal proposals.[18]

In its efforts to voice the peoples' aspirations the All-India States' Peoples' Conference had to face many heavy odds. The hostile attitude of almost all the rulers to the conference to the local organisations smothered the possibilities of the development of an effective public opinion inside the states. The extent of the princes' hostility can be easily inferred from the fact that all the conferences of the states' people were invariably held not inside the states but in the adjoining districts of British India. The British Government's attitude towards the states' peoples' organisation was one calculated to discourage its growth. It consistently refused to recognise the competence of these bodies to speak on behalf of states' people. Such a recognition would be consistent with the view expressed by many viceroys that the state governments required to be democratised. But the refusal of the British to recognise the states' peoples' organisation took away one channel of mass sanction which would have effectively entered the process of democratisation.[19]

Although the states' peoples' movement had derived its stimulus from the Indian national movement and the leader-

---

17. Jayaprakash Narayan, *Why Socialism*?, All India Congress Socialist Party, Banaras, 1936, p. 28. Narayan Achyut Patwardhan, Narendra Deva and others were the leaders of the New party.
18. *INC. RES 1934-36*, no. 28, pp. 52-53.
19. Urmila Phadnavis, op. cit. pp. 96-97.

ship of the All-India States' Peoples Conference was in the hands of some congressmen, the congress as a body was disinclined for a long time to play an active role in the Indian states. It expressed its sympathy and support to the states' people for securing the same rights for which it was struggling in British India; but at the same time it made it clear that the Congress as such would not involve itself in the struggle of these people. No wonder while the states' peoples' movement did not find the active support of the Congress in its struggle, the Congress was of immense help at the conference tables. True the All-India States' Peoples' Conference was not permitted to send its representatives to the Round Table Conferences, but it did find some congressmen acting as its spokesmen in such conferences. Also, the emphasis of the Congress on the states' peoples' right of representation in any federal scheme was a potent source of strength for the All-India States' Pooples' Conference. However, this insistence of the Congress was bound to be inacceptable to the princes and was one amongst the many other factors which obstructed the realisation of the federal part of the Government of India Act 1935.[20]

The anti-autocratic and anti-feudal agitations were emerging in some of the princely states. In Kashmir, for instance, in July 1931, where the inevitable confrontation between an overwhelming Muslim subject population and a Hindu ruling dynasty did acquire at times a certain communal tinge, but where the foundations were also being laid in these years of the powerful National Conference Movement. The agitation started by a group of Muslim graduates including Sheikh Abdullah culminated in a mass attack on the Shrinagar jail on 13 July, when 21 people were killed in the police firing. While the immediate result was a communal outburst repressive measures in September 1931 led to attacks on the police rather than on the Hindus, and the situation soon required British military intervention to help the Maharaja. In Jammu,

---

20. Ibid. p. 97.

there were anti-money-lender riots in Mirpur, Kotli and Rajansi *talukas*, and eventually the local government set up a Grievances Enquiry Commission with some non-official members on 12 November.[21]

The second phase of the Civil Disobedience Movement coincided with significant upsurges in at least two princely states.[22] In Kashmir, the concessions offered by the Grievances Enquiry Commission in April 1935 (steps to promote Muslim Education return of government occupied Muslim religious buildings, partial suspension of a grazing tax and the payments for state requisitioned labour) failed to stop a growing movement. The Muslim Conference was started in October 1932, and though it would be renamed the National conference and seven years later, its leader Sheikh Muhammad Abdullah[23] had already started to develop close contacts with a group of anti-autocratic Jamwer Hindus under P.N. Bazaz.[24]

In early 1933 in the Rajasthan State of Alwar there was a formidable rising against Maharaja Jai Singh Sawni's revenue enhancements, *begar*, grazing dues and reservation of forests for hunting. The Meos, a self-contained semi-tribal peasant community with a largely formed affinity to Islam, began a guerilla war on a large scale. On 12 February 1933 Willingdon reported the Alwar conditions to be 'getting as bad as

---

21. Sumit Sarkar, *Modern India*, p. 316.
22. Ibid. p. 324.
23. The Sheikh (born in 1905) organised the Youngmen's Muslim Association in 1930; was arrested for his political activities in September 1931 and on nine more occasions; was elected the President of Muslim Conference in October 1932. It was converted into the National Conference in 1939. In March 1948 he became the Prime Minister of Jammu and Kashmir and in 1949 joining the Constituent Assembly of India. See S.P. Sen, op, cit vol. I, p. 8.
24. Prem Nath Bazaz (born 1905) started his political career in 1930, following Mahatma Gandhi's path of non-violence to secure for Kashmir responsible government. Brought out a paper *Hamdard* to propagate nationalism, secularism, and democracy. He was arrested for xix months in 1938. See S.P. Sen, op. cit. vol I, p. 148.

they can be', and the Indian Annual Register spoke of 80-90000 Meos participating in what it predictably but mistakenly dubbed 'communal trouble'. While the Punjab Muslim leader Mohammad Yasin Khan tried to give the anti-Maharaja Movement a communal (as well as a pro-British) colour, an alternative, consciously radical trend was also developing associated with Syed Mutalabi Faridabadi, and interstingly enough, K.M. Ashraf, soon to become one of India's first Marxist historians. Eventually the British decided to pack off the unpopular Maharaja to Europe, and take over the Alwar Administration for some years.[25]

The usual princely response to this type of political activity was suppression within their own territory and requests to the British Government to choke off such opposition on its side of the border. In stead of making a bold effort to seek an accommodation with reasonable demands, the princes charged that the states' peoples' leaders were unrepresentative of the loyal masses within Princely India and their programmes were unrelated to local customs and conditions. These accusations were reminiscent of the earlier British allegations about the unrepresentative character of the leadership of the national movement. Their political shortsightedness meant that they would have to cope with increasingly belligerent demands just when their bargaining power was declining.

Simultaneously with these growing internal challenges, new opportunities arose for the princes to seek support from the arenas external to their states. The announcement of all-British composition of the Indian statutory commission in the autumn of 1927 inaugurated a new era of political confrontation and the princes were henceforth drawn into the vortex of British Indian politics.[26]

---

25. Chaudhary Abdul Haye's article in H. Kruggar (ed.), *K.M. Ashraf*, Delhi, 1969.
26. Barbara N. Ramusack, *Essay on Modern Indian History* (Ed. B.R. Nanda) p. 112.

During the first phase of the Civil Disobedience Movement (April 1930 to March 1931) the British seemed primarily concerned with securing the co-operation of the princes at the forthcoming Round Table Conference in London. The Imperial Government also tried to use some princes to reduce the muslim participation in Gandhi's current campaign. In May 1930, at the instance of the Viceroy Lord Irwin, Nizam Usman Ali Khan of Hyderabad issued a manifesto exhorting all the muslims to stand firmly aloof from the Civil Disobedience Movement.[27] The Viceroy asked the Nizam and the Nawab Hamidullah of Bhopal to exert their influence on the conservative muslim theological school of Deoband[28] to restrain the Sadr Mudarris, Hussain Ahmad Madani,[29] from continuing his vocal support to the Civil Disobedience Movement.[30] These two major patrons threatened to withdraw their annual grants to Deoband, and as a consequence the faculty persuaded their Director to undertake a pilgrimage to Mecca.[31] Apparently, the British strategy was to avoid a repetition of the Hindu-Muslim coalition of 1921 when Mahatma Gandhi had linked the Jalianwalabag firing with the Khilafat question.

---

27. Irwin to Wedgwood Benn, 25 May 1930, Political Secret, GOI, NAI.
28. As a contrast to the loyalist reformist group of the Aligarh movement of Sayyid Ahmad Khan the Deoband *Dar-ul-Ulum* (seminary) founded in 1867 by two heroes of the Revolt of 1857, Muhammad Qusim Nanawtawi and Rashid Ahmed Gangohi was a nationalist reformist group.
29. Maulana Madani (1879-1957) had joined a group of young revolutionaries in 1911-12 and in 1919 after his release from a jail in Malta, became the leader of the Jamiat-ul-Ulema-i-Hind. He participated in the Khilafat movement and was imprisoned in 1922. Leter he collaborated with the Indian National Congress and courted arrest in the Civil Disobedience Movement in 1930 and in 1932. Later in the Quit India Movement (1942) also he was jailed. See S.P. Sen (ed.), op. cit. Vol. III, p. 1.
30. Hailey to C.C. Watson, Pol. Sec. GOI, NAI.
31. Keyes to Watson, 28 February 1931, and Watson to G.B. Lambert, Governor U.P., 11 March 1931, National Archives of India (henceforth NAI), File no. 5. April. 1932.

The British Government sought the co-operation of the princes to thwart the activities of the Indian National Congress. The Bombay Presidency was particularly vulnerable to 'hit and run' activities of the Congress operating from princely territories because it contained so many 'islands' of state territories and shared long boundaries with several other states.[32] At the request of the Bombay Government the Government of India decided to solicit princely collaboration.

Initially all the political officers were instructed to ask for assistance and to ensure that special activities of the Civil Disobedience Movement such as the boycott of British goods were not allowed to be practised in their states and that their states were not used as a base for the agitation in British India.[33] Then Charles Watson, the Political Secretary, appealed to the Residents at Hyderabad and Mysore and the Agents to the Governor-General in Rajputana and Central India to ascertain if any of the rulers would be willing to issue pronouncements against the Civil Disobedience Movement. He wished that any such statement must appear to be spontaneous and should avoid giving the impression of being prompted by the government if it was to have any propaganda value.[34]

A special message was sent to the Agent to the Governor-General in Rajputana, drawing his attention to the donations made by the states' peoples to the Congress. Since finance would be a problem for the Congress in the forthcoming struggle, these states were to be requsted to bring pressure to bear upon their subjects not to make further donations to the Congress treasury.[35] While all the major Rajputana

32. Bombay Government to GOI, Home Deptt, 3 Dec. 1931. NAI, File no. 5 April 1932.
33. Watson to all Residents and Agents to the Governor-General, 7 January 1932.
34. Watson to the Residents at Hyderabad, Mysore and the Agents in Rajputana and Central India, 7 January 1932.
35. Watson to the AGG in Rajputana, 7 January 1932.

durbars responded positively to this governmental request for assistance, the Jaipur and Jodhpur governments specifically promised to take suitable action against any of their state subjects who contributed to the Civil Disobedience movement fund.[36]

Many princes responded quietly to the suggestions of their local political officers and by 29 January 1932, the Viceroy Lord Willingdon could publicly announce that 19 princes had approved governmental policies to deal with disorder and had offered to co-operate to the fullest extent with the government. The more important princes in this group were the Maharajas of Patiala, Indore, Kishangarh, Kapurthala and Jind.[37] In the following months, other prominent princes like the Nizam, the Maharaja of Kashmir, Bikaner and Bundi and the Council of Regency in Gwalior, issued their endorsement of the policies of the Government of India.[38] Not content with words, some princes such as the Maharajas of Patiala and Jodhpur imitated the Government of India in the issue of ordinances severely regulating all public meetings and presses, and rigorously punishing any who abetted any political activity.[39]

Unfortunately for harassed British officials, not all states were as quick or as ready to control the civil disobedience programmes within their borders. There were certain areas like Central India, Kathiawar and Mysore, causing great concern to British officials.

In Central India, the Maharaja Gulab Singh of Rewa pursued a conciliatory policy towards the Congress activities in his territories. Rewa was setting a 'bad' example for other states in the region as felt by the British agency. Gulab

36. R. Reynolds, AGG in Rajputana to Watson, 10 Febuary 1932.
37. *The Tribune*, 31 June 1932, p, 7.
38. Ibid., 8 June 1932, p. 15-
39. Ibid. 6 January 1932, p. 7.

Singh's 'permissiveness' was attributed to his lack of efficient and organised troops capable of dealing with the situation.[40] In May 1932, undoubtedly under British pressure and after a reorganization of his forces, the Maharaja issued restrictive ordinances, had 150 agitators arrested and got his police make lathi charge to disperse the assemblies now declared illegal by the new ordinances.[41]

The Kathiawar states were divided in their attitudes towards the Civil Disobedience Movement. Because of the interlocking pattern of their territories, this division made it difficult to contain anti-government agitations. Limbi, Morvi and Nawanagar were loyalist states pursuing a strong policy of suppression of the Congress activities. While recalcitrant states included Bhavnagar, Junagarh, Porbandar, Wadhwan and Gondal which more or less permitted the Congress to implement its programme of boycott of foreign clothes and the defiance of the Salt laws,[42] Kathiawar remained a thorn in the side of the British since it was never free from Congress agitation or sympathisers.[43]

The State of Mysore gives an insight into the varying attitudes within British officialdom. The Bombay Government complained to the Central Government that Mysore was failing to take adequate measures to cut off contributions to the Congress, that Dewan Mirza Ismail had supported Gandhi and his works, and that the Congress was permitted to maintain an office in Bangalore.[44] On a query from the Government of India, the Mysore resident advised Delhi that the

---

40. Sept. 1941 NAI, GOI. Home—Pol. 1931.
41. NAI, GOI, Home—Pol, 1932.
42. E.H. Kealey, AGG in the States of Western India to Waston, 31 January 1931.
43. NAI, GOI, Home—Pol, 1931.
44. Hallet to B.J. Glaney, Pol. Secy. GOI, 4 October 1933; Glancy to Mirza Ismail, 16 October 1933, Mirza Ismail to Glaney, 24 Oct. 1933.

Bombay Government's accusations were unfounded and therefore nothing further need to be said to the Mysore Government.[45] The Mysore resident and the more distant Government of India in New Delhi were more flexible than the hard pressed Bombay Government which had to deal more immediately with the problems of control created by the support and sympathy of the Mysore ruler with the Congress.

In certain prominent instances, the princes did not require any prodding. The two most outstanding examples in this category were the Nizam of Hyderabad and the Maharaja of Patiala. Noted throughout his long life for his miserliness despite his vast personal fortune, the Nizam of Hyderabad displayed an uncharacteristic generosity in 1930. Even though in the early part of the year he had contributed to the treasury of the Chamber of Princes, in September he offered to give privately, with no strings attached, almost twenty lakhs of rupees to the Government of India to finance the programmes to counteract the Civil Disobedience movement.[46] This gesture demonstrates the inclination of some princes to covert rather than overt participation in British Indian politics and their willingness to finance any group which might further immediate or long range objectives sought by the princes either individually or collectively.[47] Harold Wilberforce Bill, the official Political Secretary, however, deemed it prudent to decline this offer for two reasons : First, the acceptance of such a gift would make the states more directly the target of the Congress, a situation which he wished to avoid. Secondly, it would be difficult for the government to make an adequate acknowledgement of such an extraordinary gesture and it was apprehended that the Nizam might be bargaining for a relaxation of the British pressure to effect

45. Plowden to C.J. Glaney, 4 April 1934.

46. Keyes to G. Cunningham, 1 September 1930.

47. Barbara N. Ramusack, *Essay on Modern Indian History* (Ed. B.R. Nanda) p. 116.

certain political reforms.[48] Lord Irwin agreed with Wilberforce Bill's stand and the offer was gratefully declined.

Sometimes the princely involvement in British Indian politics had unforeseen result which were more distressing to the imperial patron than to its clients. One such venture was the investment by the Rulers of Nawanagar, Bhopal and Patiala in the *Bombay Chronicle*, a newspaper founded in April 1913 by Pherozeshah Mehta.[49] In early 1927 Chimanlal Setalvad[50] and Lalji Naranji two prominent moderate political figures in Bombay asked the Jam Saheb (Maharaja Ranjit Singh) of Nawanagar to extend financial support to the faltering newspaper.[51] After agreeing to do so himself, the Jam Saheb then approached the Maharaja of Patiala and they were later joined by the Nawab of Bhopal.[52] It is difficult to spell out the motivation of these princes, but one thing is clear. Since the Editor, S.A. Brelvi, was one of the two vice-chairmen of the reception committee for the All-India States' Peoples' Conference held in Bombay during December 1927, and the *Bombay Chronicle* printing press printed the papers for the Conference.[53] It might be argued that their support was yet another example of the princely preference for buying off the opposition rather than accommodating it through negotiation and reform.

In the political turmoil which followed the oppointment and Indian visit of the Simon Commission (1927) the *Bombay*

48. Note by Wilberforce-Bill, 12 Sept. 1930.
49. Mehta (1845-1915) was one of the topmost moderate leader of the Congress. He presided over the Congress Session held in Calcutta in 1890.
50. Chimanlal Harilal Setalvad (1866-1947), a friend of Pherozeshah Mehta, was a prominent lawyer and from 1899 to 1920 he represented the University of Bombay on the Bombay Municipal Corporation. He was a moderate politician.
51. Nawanagar to Irwin, 12 May 1930.
52. Patiala to Irwin, 9 May 1930 and Bhopal to Irwin, 7 May 1930.
53. Report of the Bombay Session of the Indian States' Peoples' Movement, December 1922.

Chronicle maintained a strong anti-government tone. When informed by Naoroji Dumausio of the *Times of India* about the princes' financial support to the *Bombay Chronicle*, Charles Watson warned in 1928 Nawanagar and Patiala orally about the undesirable consequences of their patronage.[54] Two years later in May 1930, Lord Irwin directly suggested to all the three princes that they call up their debentures.[55] After much discussion, the trio finally dissociated itself from the *Bombay Chronicle*.

The Maharaja of Patiala's continuing interest in the *Bombay Chronicle*, however, did not prevent him from taking a strong pro-government stand. After the Lahore Congress (December 1929) had passed the resolution calling for complete independence, Patiala used the occasion of his *Basant Panchami Durbar*[56] in February 1930 to denounce the Congress. He said, "The new attitude towards us is that the States are interpolated pages, apocryphal additions, in the history of India. I need not point out to you how this view is fundamentally opposed to the evolution of our history. To forget the persistent regionalism of our people which finds expression in the Indian States is an error which has from time to time spelt disaster for India in the past. If the nationalist movement in its desire for a symmetric pattern of Indian political life decides to act as if the States did not exist, the prospects before the whole country are gloomy indeed."[57] To make sure that he received a pat on his back for his efforts, Patiala forwarded a copy of his speech to the Political Secretary, who acknowledged it with appreciation.[58]

Two months later Patiala again intervened in the politics of British India, this time in his capacity as a leader of the

54. M. Hailey, Governor of Punjab to J. Crerar, 7 June 1928.
55. Irwin to Patiala, Bhopal and Nawanagar, 2 May 1930.
56. A Hindu festival marking the advent of the spring
57. Speech delivered by the Maharaja of Patiala on 3 February 1930.
58. patiala to Watson, 1 February 1930 and Watson to Patiala, 3 Feb. 1930.

religious sect called the Sikhism. On 6 May 1930, there was a disturbance near the Sisganj Gurudwara in old Delhi, and the Police had opened fire in an attempt to re-establish order in the area. This incident inflamed the Sikh community against the government at a time when the latter was coping with the *Salt Satyagraha*[59] launched by Mahatma Gandhi. At this critical juncture, the Maharaja of Patiala served as a mediator between the Viceroy and the elements within the Sikh community willing to seek a peaceful redress of the Sikh grievances.[60] A troublesome affair ended peacefully for the government and Patiala's position as a Sikh leader was reinforced at a time when he was under increasing attack from the Punjab Riyasati Praja Mandal, the regional states' people body, whose most active members were from the extremist faction of the Akali Dal.[61]

An analysis of the varying response made by the most active princes to the nationalist movement may not yield a clearly defined pattern but it would certainly give some insight into the thought-processes and activities of the princes.

When the Indian National Congress began to challenge the British power, the princes viewed their interests as being closely linked with their imperial patron. In most of their operations as all-India politicians these rulers supported British objectives both overtly and covertly. Apart from the defiant attitude of the Gackwad of Baroda and some Kathiawar rajas, most of the princes complied with the imperial directives asking for suppression of the Congress's non-cooperation programmes within their states. The princes were

---

59. The Mahatma had launched a peaceful protest against the government by breaking the salt law which affected the common man.
60. Leyaquat Hayat Khan to Sir Sunder Sjngh Majithia, 18 June 1930 and Arjan Shah Singh to Patiala, 16 June 1930. Sardar Sunder Singh Majithia (1872-1941) was a staunch supporter of the British India. He was decorated several times of the British Government.
61. Khuswant Singh, *A History of the Sikhs*, vol. II, p. 112.

one of the few groups within the Empire who continued to identify their goals with those of the British. There were a few instances of the princes participating in British Indian politics, pursuing the aims which were not dictated by their patron. However, neither of these princes attempted to build up a popular power base. In the sphere of politically-oriented religious groups, certain princes sought a position of leadership based on their status within a particular community. Communal leadership was a double edged sword which would cut its user as well as his enemies. While Patiala could use his standing as a Sikh leader to defend himself from the attacks by the Sikh active in the local states' peoples' movement, others such as Hyderabad, Bhopal and K ashmir found their internal positions rendered more precarious by their communal activities in British India. Even in this area, the princes frequently used their influence to further the British objectives.[62]

The princes did not make an attempt to open channels either with the Congress or with any other national group. Indeed the princes tried to ignore the burgeoning strength of the Indian nationalists. Even as the political equilibrium within their own territories was menaced by the ferment spreading in the form of the states' peoples' movement, these rulers either turned directly to the paramount power for an armed assistance or imitated the imperial repressive measure for dealing with these threats. On the appeal of the princes, the Government of India passed a more comprehensive Indian States' Protection Act in an effort to immunize their territories from the virus of political turbulence.

62. Barbara N. Ramusack in B.R. Nanda, op.cit. pp. 199-220.

3

The Princes and the Federation Plan (1931-37)

Concurrently with their efforts to establish themselves individually as effective political figures by responding to the opportunities available during the Civil Disobedience movement (1930-32), the princes also sought to secure their future along the constitutional lines. The Indian Viceroy Irwin's proposal in October 1929 that the princes should join with the Indian nationalists and the British party leaders in constitutional discussions seemed to be a major concession. Although Edwin Montagu and Lord Chelmsford during the preparation of their report of 1918 as well as the Simon Commission (1927) had consultations with the princes, they had restricted the scope of their enquiries to the matters which directly affected the states. Under the Irwin scheme, the princes were to be allowed to participate in the debate about the future constitutional arrangements for the entire subcontinent. With a long-standing attraction to the ideas of legal guarantees, the princes eagerly agreed to attend the joint talks in London for the Round Table Conferences would provide one last possibility for continued autonomy but the princes were to find it difficult to recognize what was being offered and how limited their opinions were.[1]

Much of the excitement among the princes over the proposed Round Table Conference was concentrated in the Chamber of Princes and particularly in its inner core, the standing committee. For the first time since its creation in 1921 the chamber became an active institution. The attendance increased, pertinent resolutions were debated and elections were contested. One instance of remarkable interest in the chamber was a substantial donation by the Nizam of Hyderabad to its coffers.

During the chamber sessions held in February 1930, the princes debated the Butler Committee Report which refused to define paramountcy clearly, thus limiting the scope for British intervention in their affairs. A propaganda office which had been set up in London in 1928 to promote the princely interests during the Butler Committee hearings was revived with a fresh infusion of funds.[2] The princes obviously wanted to improve their image at home and abroad. In order to lend substance to the characterization of the princes as men able to move with the times, Maharaja Ganga Singh of Bikaner pressed for the passage of a resolution reiterating their commitment to internal reforms. Most of the members present were not inclined to debate, let alone make any promises, so Bikaner's proposal fell through.[3] Despite the increasingly acrimonious attacks from a widening circle of opponents, few princes were willing to take the positive but painful steps necessary to modernize their administrations and to establish meaningful contacts with the political forces rising within their territories. Despite repeated warnings from sympathetic patrons such as Irwin, and powerful politicians such as

---

1. Ramusack in B.R. Nanda (ed.), op. cit. p. 21.
2. Proceedings of the Standing Committee of the Chamber of Princes, 21 Feb. 1930.
3. Ibid.

Motilal Nehru[4] and Madan Mohan Malviya,[5] the princes blindly persisted in their refusal to institute even moderate reforms.

The States' Peoples' organizations, meanwhile, were becoming more vocal in their attacks on maladministration and corruption in the states and in their demand of democratic reforms. The All India States' Peoples' Conference chose the opening day of the 1930 chamber session to issue a list of serious charges against the Maharaja of Patiala personally and against his administration.[6] The accusation caused considerable consternation in the British official circles and damaged Patiala's reputation.[7]

A number of short-lined inflamatory newspapers, contained vicious denunciations of the princely rule. It was difficult to stop or punish them under the provisions of the 1922 Press Protection Act. This hostile publicity campaign received further ammunition during 1929 when Popatlal Chudgar, a prominent figure in the States' Peoples' movement published a scathing, polemical book alleging general maladministration throughout princely India.[8] In an informal gathering held concurrently with the February 1930 chamber session, some princes talked about various repressive measures designed to curb such criticism. The princes' lack of concern for changing conditions which spawned such adverse comment

---

4. Motilal (1861-1931) was the President of the Allahabad branch of the Home Rule League in 1918, the President of the Amritsar session of the Indian National Congress in 1919, went to jail several times, founded the Swarajya Party in 1923 and was the President of the Committee which prepared the Nehru Report (1928).
5. Malaviya (1861-1946) was active in the Congress from its second session (1886) and was elected President of this organisation in 1909, 1918, 1932 and 1933. He was also a founder of the Hindu Mahasabha in 1906.
6. AISPC, 1930, Bombay.
7. Irwin to Wedgewood Benn Benn, 2 April 1930.
8. Popatlal Chudgar, *Indian Princes under British Protection*, p. 46.

and their preference for arbitrary controls speaks of their political orientation as they prepared to enter the deliberations on Indian constitutional reforms.[9]

Nevertheless, in the 1930 Delhi session of the chamber, some members endeavoured to renew their informal contacts with the Indian nationalists. On 26 February, the standing held a large dinner party for political leaders, most of whom did not belong to the Congress. Two days later, a smaller one took place when two liberal leaders Tej Bahadur Sapru[10] from Allahabad and Chimanlal Sitalvad from Bombay conferred with the Standing Committee and their ministerial advisers. Here it was decided to depute Kailas Nath Haksar to go to various political centres and to exchange views informally with the leaders such as C.P. Ramaswami Iyer in Madras, M.R. Jaykar and M.A. Jinnah in Bombay.[11] After the Stand-

9. *Minutes* of the meeting of the Standing Committee of the Chamber of Princes on 23 February 1930.

10. Sir Tej (1875-1949) entered active moderate politics in 1907. He was a leading lawyer. He joined the Home Rule League in 1917, but at the age of 46 he joined the Governor-General's Executive Council as a law member. He was one of the signatories to the Muddimar Reforms Committee's minority report of 1924. In 1928 he was active in the All-Parties Commiitee. At the Round Table Conference in London in 1930 he pleaded for a status of equality for India with the other self-governing dominions.

11. Meeting of the Standing Committee on 26 February, 1930. Sir C.P. Ramaswami Iyer (1879-1966) first practised law and than joined politics as a member of the Home Rule League. He was General Secretary of the Congress (1917-18). In 1920 he became the Advocate of Madras and then joined the Executive Council of the Governor-General Willingdon. He was a Law Member of the Government of India in 1931 and he was the Diwan of Travancore from 1936-47.
Jinnah (1875-1948), a lawyer by profession, was a Congress leader from 1906-20; from 1920 to 1928 he was outside the Congress; from 1928 to 1937 he changed his political complexion and from 1937 to 1947 he re-organised the Muslim League and its separatist ideas.
M.R. Jayakar (1873-1959) was a great lawyer and educationist. In the Congress session of 1917, 1918 and 1925, he made his mark as a

(*Contd.*)

ing Committee had considered Haksar's report on political currents in these areas, it was to meet again with selected politicians

The next round of discussions between the Standing Committee and the British Indian politicians took place a month later. Among those who came to Delhi to attend the meeting held on 29 March 1930, were Purshotamdas Thakurdas,[12] an industrialist, M.R. Jaykar, B.S. Moonje[13] and M.M. Malaviya, Hindu Mahasabha leaders, M.A. Jinnah and Mohammad Ali, the spokesmen for the muslim community, Hari Singh Gaur from the central provinces, Chimanlal Sitalvad from Bombay, C.P Ramaswami Aiyar from Madras, Muhammad Shafi[14] from Punjab, Ganesh Shrikrishna Khorapade[15] from Besar, and Hugh Cocke W. Arthur Moone

---

fine speaker. He was a leader of the Swarajya Party in the Bombay Legislative Council (1923-26) and in the Central Legislative he worked as the Deputy Leader of the Nationalist Party (1926-37). He participated in the London Round Table Conference and in 1937 became a Judge of the Indian Federal Court

12. Purshotamdas (1879-1961) was largely responsible for establishing the Indian Central Committee (1921) and was "the reigning Mughal" of the East India Cotton Association for over 35 years. He presided over the second session of the Indian Chamber of Commerce and Industry around 1926. In 1925 he was on the Royal Commission of Indian Finance, Currency and Practice.
13. Balakrishna Shivaram Moonje (1872-1948) was the President of the Hindu Mahasabha and a member of the Central Legislative (1926-30). He participated in the Round Table Conference in London and in 1933 in the Joint Parliamentary Committee.
14. Shafi (born in 1869) was a member of the Imperial Legislative Council in 1911, 1914 and 1917 and in 1923 he became the Vice-President of the Viceroy's Executive Council. In 1927 he presided over the Lahore Session of the Muslim League.
15. Kharpade (1854-1938) was involved in the succession case of a zamindar family in Kolhapur. He belonged to the extremist group of the Congress, a close associate of B.G. Tilak. In 1920 he left the Congress and got elected to the Central Legislative Assembly which he served till 1925.

and D'Arcy Lindsay, the non-official European members of the Legislative Assembly.[16] They were willing to go to Delhi in heat of late March since many of them still thought, as did Setalvad, that "conversations with the Princes" were very important.[17]

Bhupinder Singh of Patiala opened the proceedings of asking what the attitude of a dominion status government would be towards the states. Most of the British Indian leaders present were prompt to assure the princes that there would be a greater degree of cooperation between a dominion government in British India and the states than existed under the present management.[18] Malaviya promised the establishment of such institutions as a supreme court and a machinery for co-operation in common affairs such as defence, and he declared further that the princes would not be forced to adapt any prescribed form of government. To work out the details for a united India D'Arcy Lindsay, the leader of the European members in the Assembly, suggested the appointment of an appropriate committee. Ramaswami Aiyar, Mohammad Ali, Gour, Shafi, Haksar and Manubhai Mehta were designated for such a body, but the committee never met.[19]

Though these informal conversations between certain princes and Indian politicians did not produce any tangible results, they indicated the relationship existing between these two groups on the eve of the Round Table Conference. Besides, among the politicians who maintained contacts with the princes a prominent majority also had ties with communal political organisations such as the Muslim League and the Hindu Mahasabha.

---

16. Ibid.
17. Setalvad to Sapru, 10 March 1930.
18. Meeting of 29 March 1930.
19. Note by S.K. Fitze of his conversation with Haksar on 1 August 1930.

Along with the princes and the British Indian politicians, the officials of the highest levels of the British Government were working behind the scenes in London and in Delhi to solve the problems raised by their invitations to the Indian princes to participate in constitutional debates.

On the thorny issue of the composition of the Indian States' delegation, the Viceroy faced two difficulties. Various spokesmen for the States' Peoples' groups had petitioned Irwin as well as Indian politicians, pleading for representation at the conference. On the same day that he had made his announcement on the dominion status, Irwin had advised Vithalbhai Patel, the President of the Central Legislative Assembly, that representatives of the All India States' Peoples' Conference would have no *locus siandi* at the conference. The discussion would focus on the relationship between British India and the Indian states and only the accredited governments of the states, as represented by the princes, could speak with authority.[20]

Supporting Delhi's position on this question, Wedgewood Benn, the Secretary of State for India, reasoned, "our prime objective is to make the conference a success. Merely on the grounds of tactics, therefore,......it would be fatal to alienate the princes."[21] Notwithstanding this attitude the Secretary of State also advocated that some conciliatory gesture be made to the States' Peoples' movement : a leading prince, through the prompting of the political department, if necessary, should announce some major advance in the direction of progressive political reform. He argued that it would be better for the Viceroy to pursue a policy of general encouragement of the representative institutions in the states, rather than confine himself in issuing paternal warnings in individual cases of maladministration.[22]

20. Irwin to Wedgewood Benn, 5 Nov. 1929.
21. Wedgewood Benn to Irwin, 13 Nov. 1929.
22. Wedgewood Benn to Irwin, 12 Dec. 1929.

After the officers in the Secretariat of the political department had spent a couple of weaks studying the previous viceregal efforts to encourage positive reforms, Irwin vetoed the proposal from London. His argument was that such a step would accomplish little among the States' Peoples' groups and might unduly frighten the princes at a crucial juncture.[23] It was to be tragic for the princes that the British officials most directly charged with their future preferred to obscure the need for drastic political reforms and an accommodation with the newly rising political elites within their states. At this point the government needed allies at the Round Table Conference and even Lord Irwin, who began his term as a strong advocate of the reform, declined to take any action which might antagonize the princes, the long standing clients of the British government.

The position of the government on the representation of the states' peoples' groups was reinforced by the opinion of these Indian politicians who were most anxious for the triumph of the constitutional reforms and methods. In a private letter to Sapru, B.L. Mitter, the Law Member of Irwin's Executive Council, supported the viceroy's position.[24] Setalvad independently argued as did Wedgewood Benn that "it would be most unwise and a great tactical blunder for us to call in representatives of the states subjects. The moment we do that we destroy all chances of the All India Constitution, and unless they are prepared to negotiate we will come to a standstill."[25]

Although the above question was quickly settled to the satisfaction of the princes, they were not yet content. There was still the troublesome issue of who would be included on the state delegation. Throughout February and March 1930, the Standing Committee lobbied with Irwin and the political

---

23. Irwin to Wedgewood Benn, 12 Jan. 1930.
24. Mitter to Sapru, 20 Nov. 1929.
25. Setalvad to Sapru, 13 Feb. 1930.

department to ensure that delegates recommended by it were nominated.[26] The most disgruntled ruler at this time was the Nizam who felt that the chamber had neglected to consult him at all stages, failing to give him adequate representation despite his high status in the Princely India. The Nizam's plea for a separate representation was enthusiastically supported by Terence Keyes, the British Resident at Hyderabad, who was a staunch opponent of Harcourt Butler's concept of two Indians—a British India and an Indian India ruled by the princes and a firm champion of the federation as the best means of preserving the British creation of an Indian nation.[27]

The Indian states' delegation consisted of sixteen members. The delegates included the members of the Standing Committee of the chamber and two ministers nominated by the committee—Manubhai Mehta from Bikaner and Kailash Nath Haksar from Gwalior. The latter was appointed the Secretary-General of the delegation.

By the end of October most members of the states' delegation had arrived in London. The members of the delegation had leisurely talks with the politicians of British India in the ship while coming to London. This dialogue during the voyage provided a major channel of communication between the two groups.[28] It must be noted, however, that this was a logical follow-up of the informal gatherings which had been taking place for the past two years whenever the members of the Standing Committee assembled in Delhi.

After their arrival in London, a committee of ministers was appointed in November to consider what attitude the princes should adopt if a federal scheme of government for the whole sub-continent was proposed by the British Indian

---

26. A note by R.R. Das of the Chamber Secretariat, 11 June 1930.
27. Keyes to Watson, 15 April 1930.
28. D.A. Low (ed.), *Soundings in Modern South Asian History*, Berkeley, 1978, p. 315.

delegation. If the committee favoured the proposal, it was also to suggest what safeguards the princes should demand before acceding to such a federal scheme.[29] The committee strongly advocated the acceptance of a federal proposal, and its recommendations were endorsed by a larger committee under the chairmanship of the Nawab of Bhopal. This latter group argued that the Simon Commission Report of 1930 was inadequate since it contained no provision for a princely voice in the settlement of the matters of common concern. Therefore, unless the states joined with British India in a federation to share in any further devolution of power, they would be placed at a great disadvantage as British India alone would gain in power.[30]

Many factors influenced the princes and their ministers to take this decision. As early as 1918, the more politically astute among them had begun to ask for some form of joint co-operation with British India.[31] By the time of their 1927 conference with Irwin, they were talking of some type of federation. Though wary of a full political union, they were attracted to the idea of an economic confederation with a political link to facilitate discussion on pressing political matters. At the time of the Butler Committee Enquiry, Leslie Scott, the chief counsel for the chamber's special organization, had formulated proposals for the establishment of certain joint institutions such as a supreme court. These proposals were never formally presented to the government, as the terms of reference of the Butler Committee precluded any discussion on the future developments. Though there had been little concrete thinking about the structure and implications of a possible federation, the word itself, by 1930, was current in the princely vocabulary. Many rulers viewed the acceptance of a federation

---

29. The Committee of the States' Secretariat at the Round Table Conference, 1931.
30. Ibid.
31. K.M. Pannikar, *His Highness the Maharaja of Bikaner*, p. 11.

as one more stage in the advancement of their vague aspirations for joint institutions with British India.

Then again after the disappointing report of the Butler Committee, a sizeable number of princes were increasingly anxious to limit the prerogatives of political officers. To many of them, federation seemed to be a device which would drastically reduce the power of the Political Department of the British Indian government in the states which would be the federal units and consequently would enjoy direct access to the central executive and legislature. As Malcolm Hailey, who attended the final Round Table conference, as the representative of the Government of India, later remarked, "They, the princes, seem to be out for the extinction of the Political Department, rather than the creation of a Federal Constitution."[32]

The princes were also under constant and persuasive pressure from Tej Bahadur Sapru, a leading proponent of federation, and his close political and personal friend, Kailas Nath Haksar. During the months preceding the Round Table Conference, Sapru and other Indian politicians devoted to constitutional processes, were in a quandary. While the Congress was now demanding complete independence, neither the Simon Report nor the Government of India's recommendations on the Report conceded any major devolution of power within the central government. It appeared to Sapru that responsible government at the centre was the minimum advance necessary to keep India within the British Empire.[33] A federation between British India and Princely India, with the latter acting as a conservative counter-weight to the radical elements in the former section, was the device by which the British parliament might be persuaded to grant central

32. Hailey to Irwin, 19 November 1930.

33. D.A. Low (ed.), op. cit, *Sir Tej Bahadur Sapru and the First Round Table Conference*, pp. 302-318.

responsibility.[34] As the Secretary-General of the Indian States' Delegation, Haksar, who shared Sapru's views was able to ensure that the federation proposals would be displayed in the most flattering light possible at the meetings of the delegation.

After months of intense preparations ranging from the efforts by Sapru to establish rapport between Mahatma Gandhi and the government to the construction by the British Ministry of the works of a special oral table, capable of accommodating all the delegates. George V inaugurated the Round Table Conference in London on 12 November 1930. While the opening ceremony seemed lacking in the pageantry associated with the imperial *durbar*, the king uttered his words of welcome into a silver and gold microphone, which relayed the imperial message throughout the world.[35] It was a gesture appropriately symbolic of a new era in imperial relations. The first plenary session of the conference opened on 17 November 1930 with an opening address by Sir Tej who appealed to the princes to join an all-India federation. He maintained that the association of the Indian states with British India would be welcome for three reasons :

1. they would furnish a stabilising factor in a federal constitution;
2. the process of unification would begin at once; and
3. in regard to matters of defence, the states would provide British India with the practical experience which it would lack.[36] Sir Muhammad Shafi and M.A. Jinnah, representing the Muslim League, also supported an all-India a federation.

---

34. T.B. Sapru to P.N. Sapru, 19 Nov. 1930; Sapru to Palanpur, 28 November 1930.
35. *The Times*, 13 November 1930, p. 12.
36. Indian Round Table Conference, *Proceedings*, 12 November 1930—19 January 1931, His Majesty's Stationary Office, London, 1932, p. 29.

Accepting the invitation of British India, the Maharaja of Bikaner said that the princes agreed that an all-India federation was "likely to prove the only satisfactory solution of India's problem,"[37] and that the princes were prepared to contribute "to the evolution of a system of government which will lead to the close and effective association of Indian states with British India."[38] But he made it clear that they would come to such a federation only "on terms of which will secure the just rights of their states and subjects."[39] Enumerating these terms, the Maharaja of Patiala stated that the continuance of the British connection, the safeguard of their treaty rights and the preservation of their internal autonomy without any interference from British India were the basis of their stand. He also elaborated the concept of federation which the princes had in mind. To the princes, the federation was "an arrangement entered into by us and by British India jointly under which, while British India manages those affairs which exclusively concern it, and while the crown discharges such functions as are reserved to it, the crown, British India and the Indian states join together in a system which provided for the joint management and joint control of matters that jointly concern the two sides of India."[40]

The acceptance of an all-India federation by the princes was acclaimed as a great achievement of the conference. In order to thrash out the details of such a federation it was decided to appoint several committees to deal respectively with the different aspects of the questions like the federal structure, defence, etc. In all such committees, the princes had adequate representation.[41]

With the appointment of these committees, the work of the first Round Table Conference seemed to be over. In a

---

37. Ibid., p. 37.
38. Ibid.
39. Ibid.
40. Ibid., p. 79.
41. Ibid., pp. 200-99 and 399-402.

declaration on behalf of the British Government, on 19 January 1931, the Prime Minister, noted the following points as emerging from the deliberations of the conference. These were :

1. the centre should be a federation of India embracing both the Indian states and British India;
2. the precise form and structure of the government must be determined after further discussions with the princes and the representatives of British India;
3. with regard to all the matters not ceded by them to the federation, the states will be related with the crown acting through the Agency of the Viceroy;
4. the defence and external affairs will be the special responsibility of the Governor-General;
5. the Governor-General will have special powers to deal with an emergency in order to maintain the tranquility of the states.[42]

However, in view of the character of the conference, the British Government decided to adjourn it at this juncture so that Indian opinion could be consulted upon the work done by the conference. The government also promised that if the non-cooperating section of the British Indian politicians, who were carrying on the civil Disobedience Movement, desired to co-operate, "steps will be taken to enlist their services."[43]

With the end of the first Round Table Conference began the quest for federal constitutional structure. In this quest, the states were faced with two difficult problems : first, to evolve a formula for the representation of a large number of small states in the federal structure, and secondly, to effect a reconciliation between the safeguards which they had demand-

42. Ibid., pp. 505-6.
43. Ibid., p. 508.

ed and the character of the federation which the British Indian statesmen had in mind.[44]

The rulers of the small states felt much concerned with the question of the distribution of the seats among the states in the federal legislature. All of them insisted on adequate representation and some of them maintained that their acceptance or refusal of the federal scheme was dependent solely on whether they were given individual representation or not. Besides, the states like Panna and Malerkotla even expressed grave doubts on the "wisdom and practicality"[45] of accepting an all-India federation.

The rulers of small states found a powerful supporter of their case in the Maharaja of Patiala. In a pamphlet published in June 1931[46] he expressed his preference for a 'united states in relationship to the crown' to a federation of the Indian states and British India. He thought that there was no "trace of federal spirit in India." He further maintained that with the implementation of the federal scheme the smaller states were bound to disappear, because the federation could not compromise such a vast number of states as its units. No attempt, he said, was made to safeguard the interests of the federal units in the face of the powers of a strong federal executive and no device had been suggested in the scheme to minimise the chances of "conflicts of interests and power" between the units and the centre. Finally, he pointed out that "paramountcy would continue to be exercised by the representatives of the crown in the same arbitrary and unreasonable manner." He viewed the future of the states as "dark, uncertain and gloomy under the federal constitution."[47]

---

44. Urmila Phadnavi, op. cit. p. 59.
45. IV (b) 17 of 1931, Patiala Archives Chamber Section, NAI, pp. 40-4.
46. The Maharaja of Patiala, *Federation and Indian States*, Thacker Spink and Co., Simla, 19з1, p. 12.
47. Ibid., pp. 13-14.

On the basis of these objections, the Maharaja of Patiala proposed an alternative scheme for a Union of States and, in fact, believed that the nucleus of such a union already existed in the chamber of princes. To make it broadbased, he suggested that the chamber should be enlarged to provide individual representation to those rulers who had the right to send only twelve representatives so far and to provide some sort of representation to those who were not represented at all in the chamber.[48] This reconstituted chamber should have an enlarged standing committee with powers to confer with the permanent standing committee of both legislatures of British India specially constituted for the purpose and settle with it "all the questions of common interest and policy." In the case of any dispute or disagreement, all justiciable issues should be referred to the judicial committee of the Privy Council in England and all non-justiciable issues should be decided by a permanent court of Arbitration comprising the representatives of the two parties and presided over by a representative on the crown.[49]

The Patiala scheme of the union of states differed from Simon's suggestion of a Council of Greater India in as much as while the former contemplated two separate standing committees, the latter envisaged a single council. The Patiala scheme also differed from the scheme prepared by the Maharaja of Dholpur. Unlike the former, the latter envisaged an all-India federation of the states and British India through the confederation of states.[50] On 9 August 1931 the Maharaja of Patiala and Dholpur met the Rulers of Panna and Jhalwar at Bombay and evolved a agreed scheme which came to be known as Dholpur-Patiala scheme.[51]

The scheme envisaged a federation constituted by British India and "Confederation of States", i.e., the "Indian States

48. Ibid.
49. Ibid.
50. IV (b) 24 of 1931, Patiala Archives, NAI.
51. III (c) 29 of 1931, Ibid.

collectively", as federating units. This confederation was to comprise :

1. the states whose rulers were members of the chamber of princes, and
2. collective representations of the remaining states.[52]

The confederation would deal with all federal matters including the election of the state representatives as well as the question of due representation of its units in the federal legislature. Secondly, the confederation would function "through the chamber of Princes, suitably enlarged both in respect of its numerical strength and scope."[53] Finally, in the cases of "breach of or non-compliance on the part of any state, the confederation [Chamber of Princes] will take the responsibility"[54] to see that decisions of the Federal Government were properly enforced.

The Dholpur-Patiala scheme differed from the Patiala scheme on two major points. First, while the Patiala scheme attacked the idea of a federarion for India, the revised scheme accepted an all-India federation for "the purpose of specified matters of common concern only", and accepted the confederation of states as a medium for their entering into all-India federation with British India. In other words, the confederation was a step prior to federation.[55] Secondly, while, in the Patiala scheme all the states entitled to send representatives to the chamber of princes were to be admitted to it as its permanent members, in the Dholpur-Patiala scheme they were to be combined in groups for the purpose of their association with the chamber. Thirdly, the powers and functions assigned to the standing committee of the enlarged chamber of princes in the Patiala scheme were denied to it in

52. Foreign and Political Department no. 21, Special, 1931, pp. 58-60.
53. Ibid. p. 59.
54. Ibid.
55. IV (b) 17 of 1931, Patiala Archives.

the Dholpur-Patiala scheme. Fourthly, unlike the Patiala scheme, the new one rendered the chamber responsible for the enforcement of the decisions of the federal government in the case of non-compliance by a state and to select the representatives of the states in the federal legislature. Both the schemes, however, laid equal emphasis on a necessity of enlarging the chamber of princes and making it equally representative of the smaller states. The smaller states naturally welcomed such a scheme as it was favourable to them and also because it satisfied their prestige.[56]

Twenty-nine rulers[57] belonging to the confederation school met in Bombay on 28 August 1931,[58] and resolved to send one confederationist in the Indian states' delegation to put forward their views before the Round Table Conference and the Federal Structure Committee.[59] The scheme soon began to attract more rulers who signified their consent to the declaration which was sent to them for their approval. Twenty states gave their assent to the scheme six more had promised to join the confederation and thirty-six states expressed their leanings towards the scheme.[60] Thus, more than ninety states, including certain middle-sized states like Patiala, Indore, Jodhpur, and Rampur, decided to refuse to accept any constitution which involved *inter alia* (1) the creation of a new state and the consequent imposition of uniform nationality and double allegiance on the subjects of states; (2) the infringement of the rights, privileges and prerogatives of the rulers of the Indian states; (3) any infringement of the treaties, *sanads* and engage-

---

56. Ibid.
57. Rulers of Bhavnagar, Bijawar, Banswara, Cambay, Danta, Dholpur, Dewas, Dharampur, Idar, Indore, Joara, Jodhpur, Junagadh, Limbdi, Lunawade, Morvi, Muthal, Orchha, Panna, Pratapgarh, Patiala, Porbandar, Rajgarh, Rampur, Sachin, Sangli, Sonepur and Tehrigarhwal participated.
58. IV (a) 14 of 1931, Patiala Archives
    I (b) 21 of 1931, p. 44
59. Ibid.
60. IV (c) 29 of 1931, Patiaia Archives.

ments of the Indian states without the consent of the states concerned, or which subordinated in any manner the Indian states to the legislative authority of the Imperial parliament or which did not secure *inter alia* (a) adequate and individual representation in the federal legislature for all stores whose rulers were or might become the members of the chamber of princes, in their own right or of the groups of remaining states, (b) the preservation of Indian states as a separate entity, or (c) the maintenance of the complete internal autonomy of the states and the reservation of all residuary powers with them. According to these rulers, the federal authority was to exercise legislative and executive powers with respect to only such subjects as might be specified with "the individual consent of all states."[61] The Dholpur-Patiala scheme was endersed to the extent it was calculated to fulfil these objectives.

The emergence of the confederationists divided the princes into two groups—the Bikaner-Bhopal group, which favoured joining the federation directly, and the Dholpur-Patiala group which favoured joining the federation through confederation. Though attempts had been made meanwhile to bring these two groups to terms in the conference held in Bombay from 30 June to 3 July, and though apparently the Federationists agreed that the "door to federation or confederation should be left open."[62] Yet the inconclusive discussions among the Federationists and confederationists during the period when the sessions of the Federal Structure Committee was on, made it clear that such an understanding was superficial and unworkable and that the differences between the two were largely a reflection of the conflict between the interests of the smaller states and those of the bigger ones.

---

61. IV (b) 25 of 1931, Patiala Archives Chamber Section.
(c) 21 of 1931.

62. Ibid.

The Federal Structure Committee, which was also attended by Mahatma Gandhi as the sole representative of the Indian National Congress, met on 7 September 1931, prior to the Second Round Table Conference. The states' delegation to the committee was strengthened by the inclusion of the rulers of Baroda, Rewa, Dholpur and Sangli.

In the meeting of the Federal Structure Committee held on 24 September 1931, the ruler of Dholpur explained the confederation scheme and its merits.[63] Tej Bahadur Sapru, however, raised many questions regarding the scheme such as the number of states joining it and the time its materialisation would take. Wondering whether the formation of an electroral college would "at all be a workable and feasible scheme", he wanted to know whether the states would agree to permit the task to be performed for them by the chamber of princes. He felt convinced that by accepting the confederationist scheme the princes would be "Imposing upon themselves a super-sovereign in the person of the chamber to princes" and held that the scheme "would not facilitate the creation of a federation which we have in view." The scheme, however, did not evoke much enthusiasm among the British Indian delegation.[64]

The Second Round Table Conference was almost entirely dominated by Gandhi, who was not opposed to the federation idea. He was, however, against dyarchy at the centre even for a transitional period. He claimed complete control over defence and external affairs and insisted that a responsible government at the centre must be established in full and at once. Unfortunately the British Government did not accept Gandhi's demand.[65] At the end of the conference, the British Premier reaffirmed that "the great idea of an all-India federa-

---

63. Indian Round Table Conference (Second Session), proceedings of the Federal Structure Committee and the Minorities Committee, His Majesty's Stationery Office, London, 1932, pp.518-9.
64. Ibid. p. 134.
65. V.P. Menon, *The Integration of the Indian States*, p.30.

tion still holds the field. The principle of a responsible federal government, subject to certain reservations and safeguards through a transition period remains unchanged."[66]

The communal problem and the division among the princes also foredoomed the federation. The main lines of cleavage were in regard to the representation of the states in the federal legislature and the financial liabilities of the federating states. As regards representation, there were three main divisions. The major states, notably Hyderabad, Mysore and Baroda, demanded representation in proportion to their importance and population. The Maharaja of Bikaner favoured an upper house of two hundred and fifty, with a fifty per cent representation for the states, so that all the members of the chamber of princes might have a seat. He was ready to offer one or two additional seats to the major states as a sop. On the other hand, Maharaja of Patiala continued to sponsor a scheme for a confederation of the states as a first step towards federation.[67]

As regards finance, the Federal Structure Sub-committee's findings destroyed the hope that the rulers could gain any financial profit by joining the federation.[68] The apprehension that the states might probably have to contribute more, and not less, towards the all-India expenditure, that federal agencies might function in the states, and that the Federal Supreme Court might gradually extend its jurisdiction over the state's subjects disillusioned the rulers of any fancy that they would be the gainers by joining the federation. Sir Mirza Ismail informed the conference that Mysore would not join the federation unless relieved of the liability of paying the tribute.

---

66. Indian Round Table Conference (Second Session), *Proceedings of the Plenary sessions*, 7 September 1931, 1 December 1931, Central Publication Branch, Calcutta, 1932, p. 291.
67. V.P. Menon, op. cit. p.31.
68. Raghubir Singh, *Indian States and the New Regime*, Taraporewala, Bombay, 1938, 1939.

Sir Akbar Hydari suggested that unless the Nizam's wishes in regard to Berar were satisfied, Hyderabad would stand out; Baroda demanded satisfaction on the port Okha and salt questions before business could be done, and so on. The rulers gradually started turning their backs on federation and the outlook at the conclusion of the Second Round Table Conference was far from roseate. Some of the rulers now began to hope that nothing would come out of the conference and that they would be able to continue their sheltered existence while the Hindus and the Muslims pursued their differences in British India.[69]

The Indian princes rejected the scheme of federation. Their apprehension was : if the British withdrew from India, their states would be absorbed, their titles abolished and their privileges and personal power subjected to the will and whim of the rulers of free India. Most of them, therefore, displayed little enthusiasm for any scheme for freedom.[70]

The third and last session of the Round Table Conference assembled on 17 November 1932. It was smaller than its predecessors; only forty-six delegates attended. Most of the states were represented by two ministers—Sir Manubhai Mehta and Sir Liaquat Hyat Khan—who were deputed by the chamber of princes. Sir Akbar Hydari and Sir Mirza Ismail were there, as were most of the British Indian delegates, but none of the important rulers was present. Moreover, the opposition Labour Party refused to take part in the conference. The serious gap at this session, as at the first, was the absence of the Congress, for meanwhile it had launched another campaign of Civil Disobedience.[71] The important question considered at this short session was the composition of the federal legislature. The form of the states' instrument of accession to the federation was also discussed. As they

69. V.P. Menon, op. cit. p. 31.
70. D.C. Gupta, *Indian National Movement*, p. 161.
71. V.P. Menon, op. cit. p. 31.

were not at all to be satisfied by any sort of compromise, the Secretary of State wisely decided not to waste time of the conference on "profitless wranglings amongst ourselves."

The third Round Table Conference could not settle the size of the federal chambers, the proportion of British Indian and states' representation and all the allocation of the states' seats. Another issue on which the princes were not at all prepared to compromise was federal finance. The more the scheme crystallised the more they began to realise that the proposed federation might be a liability rather than an asset to them.[72]

In March 1933 the proposals of the British government, in the light of the three sessions of the Round Table Conference and the subsequent negotiations, were published in a White Paper which proposed a Federation of India which was to be a "union" the Governors' provinces and the federating states.[73] This federation could be established by a proclamation of the British Crown on a request by both the Houses of Parliament. Such a request could, however, be made only when the rulers of the Indian states representing not less than half the aggregate population of these states and entitled to not less than half the seats allotted to the states in the upper chamber had signified their desire to accede to the federation.[74] The ruler was to accede to the federation by an Instrument of Accession whereby he would transfer to the crown for the purposes of federation his powers and jurisdiction in respect of those matters which he would be willing to recognise as federal matters.[75] In the case of every state which would accede, the powers and jurisdiction of the federation in relation to that state and its subjects were to be strictly

---

72. Urmila Phadnavis, op. cit. p. 70.
73. *Proposals for Indian Constitutional Reform*, Government of India Press, 1933, Delhi, p.31.
74. Ibid. p.32.
75. Ibid. p.31.

coterminus with the powers and jurisdiction transferred to the crown by the ruler himself and defined in his Instrument of Accession. All the powers of the crown in relation to the states which were to be exercised by the Governor-General-in-Council, were to be exercised by the viceroy as the crown's representative.[76]

The federal legislature was to be bicameral. In the council of states (the upper chamber), the states were provided not more than 100 out of 200 seats and in the federal assembly they were to have not more than 125 seats out of 375.[77] The representatives of the states in the federal legislature were to be 'appointed' by their rulers.[78]

The proposals of the White Paper did not evoke the enthusiasm of the princes. The confederationist group expressed its disappointment at the White Paper's silence on the question of the confederation. To the chamber of the princes also the proposals were unacceptable.[79] However, the chamber resolved to make a further attempt toward that end in view of the reasonable amendment promised by the viceroy.[80]

In April 1933, a Joint Select Committee of both the Houses of Parliament was appointed under the chairmanship of Lord Linlithgow to consider the future of the government of India with special reference to the White Paper proposals.[81] The committee was authorized to consult with the delegates

---

76. Ibid.
77. Ibid. p. 36.
78. Ibid. p. 2.
79. Chamber of Princes Proceedings of the informal meeting of the ruling princes held at Delhi in March 1933.
80. Proceedings of the Chamber of the Princes 1933, Government of India Press, Delhi, 1933, p. 34.
81. Joint Committee on Indian Constitutional Reforms (Session 1933-34), vol. I, Part I, Report, His Majesty's Stationery Office, London 1934, p. v.

from British India and the states. The standing committee of the chamber deputed P.K. Sen, Mir Maqbool and K.M. Pannikar[82] to give evidence before the committee. The Congress was still in the wilderness and did not participate in these discussions. The Joint Select Committee submitted its report in October 1934.

While on a majority of matters it merely endorsed the recommendations of the White Paper, it laid special emphasis on the voluntary character of the accession of the states to the federation.

On 12 December 1934, a motion that a Bill based on the committee's report should be submitted to the parliament was carried in the House of Commons; and on 19 December the Government of India Bill was introduced. The chamber of princes appointed fifteen states' ministers under the chairmanship of Akbar Hydari to examine the bill. The committee observed that "in some important respects the Bill departs from the agreed position arrived at during the meetings of the states' representatives with His Majesty's Government."[83] It pinpointed that the Instrument of Accession was not in the form of a "bilateral agreement between the states and the crown" and did not include "any declaration or covenant on the part of His Majesty preserving inviolate the treaties and agreements concluded with the states."[84] It also suggested

82. Pannikar was a famous administrator, diplomat and historian who had written a book on the Dyarchy under the Montagu-Chelmsford reforms under the pseudonym 'Keralaputra'.

83. Views of Indian States : Correspondence relating to a meeting of States' Rulers held at Bombay to discuss the Government of India Bill and a provisional draft Instrument of Accession, Government of India Press, Delhi, 1935, p.3.

84. Ibid p.10.

that the Instrument of Accession should indicate in a schedule "the matter in respect of which the states agreed to federate and the reservations, conditions and limitations to which they acceded."[85] It concluded that without satisfactory amendments on the lines indicated the proposed scheme could not be accepted by the rulers.[86]

A further conference of rulers and states' representatives was held in Bombay in February 1935 when it was resolved that 'the Bill and the Instrument of accession do not secure those vital interests and fundamental requisites of the states on which they have throughout laid great emphasis.'[87] They pointed out that the success of further negotiations in relation to the scheme of federation would depend entirely upon the extent to which the British Government were prepared to accept those modifications.[88] The rulers of Patiala, Bhopal and Bikaner addressed a note to the Viceroy detailing certain amendments.

The Secretary of State gave careful consideration to the views of the rulers and circulated through the viceroy, a memorandum examining in detail the specific points raised. It was made clear that it was not the intention of the British Government at that stage to seek from the rulers an undertaking to enter into federation or to discuss new matters which had no bearing on the form of the bill. It was agreed, however, that the legal advisers of the rulers could meet the parliamentary draftsmen and discuss any points at issue.[89]

---

85. Ibid.
86. Ibid. p.3.
87. Views of Indian States; Correspondence relating to a Meeting of States' Rulers held at Bombay to discuss the Government of Indian Bill and a Provisional Draft Instrument of Accession, Government of India Press, Delhi, 1933, 1.11.
88. Ibid.
89. V.P. Menon, op. cit. p.34.

The Bill became an act after receiving the royal assent on 4 August 1935.

The Federal Scheme of 1935 : The federal scheme embodied in the Government of India Act, 1935 was the first effort to provide for a constitutional relationship between the Indian states and the Government of India on a federal basis. One of the specific features of this scheme was that, whereas in the case of the provinces accession to federation was to be automatic, in the case of the states the accession was to be voluntary and the establishment of the contemplated federation was conditional on the accession of the states entitled to fill not less than one-half of the total population of the states.[90]

A state was considered to have acceded when its ruler executed an instrument of accession and after it was accepted by the British crown. The instrument would empower the federal government, the federal legislature, the federal court and any other federal authority to exercise in relation to the states such functions as might be vested in them by or under the Act; but the authority to perform such functions was to be exercised only in respect of these matters accepted by the ruler as federal in his instrument of accession and subject to such limitations as might be specified in it. Though accession was to be voluntary, the rulers were expected to accede on the first forty-seven items of the federal legislative list including the item relating to fees in respect of the matters so accepted, and the content of accession was to be uniform as possible for all states.[91]

The federal legislature was to make laws for a federated state only in matters enumerated for this purpose in the Instrument of Accession, and subject to such limitations, if

---

90. *Government of India Act, 1935*, Government of India Press, Delhi, 1936, Section 5 (2).

91. V.P. Menon, op. cit. p.35.

any, which were impossed by that Instrument.[92] Thus unlike the provinces, a federated state was to have residuary powers; and could also have concurrent jurisdiction in respects of federal subjects so enumerated in the Instrument of Accession, but, of course, subject to the overriding power of the Federal Legislature.[93]

In the executive field too, the authority of the federation, in its application to the states, was to be correspondingly circumscribed.[94] The executive authority of the federation was further sought to be limited by the reservation of executive power by the rulers in their Instrument of Accesssion authorised in the section 8(1) and (2) of the Act.[95] This implied the introduction into the Act of a theory of division of powers in thc federal sphere itself.[96] This was an arrangement patently anti-federal in the sense that it was utterly contrary to the principle of division of powers, legislative, executive and judicial, found in every other federal constitution.

In the fiscal field also, there was no uniformity as between the states and the provinces. The states were required to accede on a very limited number of items such as customs and excise duties and corporation and salt tax. Even in this field, there was a concession to the demands made by the states that they should contribute to the federal fisc in the form of indirect taxes only, enabling the states to pay appropriate contribution in lieu of taxes such as Corporation Tax.[97] The unevenness of the financial burden was inevitable in a set-up in which some of the federating units retained control

---

92. *The Government of India Act, 1935*, Section 6(2).
93. *White Paper on Indian States*, p.25.
94. Ibid.
95. *The Government of India Act, 1935*, Section 8(1) (2).
96. *White paper on Indian States*, p.25.
97. *The Government of India Act, 1935*, Section 139.

over federal subjects such as the armed forces and the railways etc.

In the judicial field also the jurisdiction of the federal court over the states, was extremely limited. Internal constitution of the states was no concern of the framers of the scheme of 1935. An order of the federal court to any judicial or civil authority of a federated state would be in the form of a letter of request to its ruler.[98]

Under the Act, federated states were assigned a considerable weightage in the matter of distribution of seats in the Federal Legislature, while the population of the Indian states did not constitute even one quarter of the total population of India, the states were allotted 104 out of 260 seats in the council of states, and 125 out of 375 seats in the Federal Assembly.[99] The representatives of British India were to be elected, but the representative of the states were to be nominated by their rulers.[100] The relationship of the rulers with the paramount power was safeguarded by creating a Crown Representative in addition to the Governor-General. While the functions of the crown in relation to British India and the federation were to be exercised by the Governor-General, its functions relating to the states, including that of paramountcy were to be exercised by the Grown Representative.[101] It meant that paramountcy would not be transferred to the federation.

That was not all. The states were free to join or not to join the federation. And everybody knew that the bigger states like Hyderabad and Kashmir would never yield. The federation could not be created until a sufficient number of states had joined it to ensure that half the states' quota of

98. Ibid. Section 211.
99. Ibid. Section 18.
100. S.R. Mehrotra, op. cit. p.242.
101. *The Government of India Act, 1935*, no. 1, Section 3.

seats had been filled in the supper house and half the population of the states had been included. This was a condition almost impossible to be fulfilled. The states were thus given a veto over the question of federation. The friends of the princes in Britain, Winston Churchill and others, had got a promise from the British Government that the princes would not be coerced, and unless the princes were coerced they would not join the federation.[102]

Thus the scheme of 1935 lacked the essential elements of a federal constitution. Lord Meston rightly likened this scheme to the 'mixing of oil with water'. It was indeed no more than a marktime plan which, had it been adopted, might or might not have paved the way for a full-fledged federal project.[103] "Could this gigantic quill of jumbled catch work, as Winston Churchill called it, really function ?" As S. R. Mehrotra remarks, "the Government of India Act, 1935 was not only meant to work, it was in fact unworkable."[104]

Lord Linlithgow [105] came to India in 1936 as the viceroy and Governor-General fired with the ambition to inaugurate the federation as early as possible. He thought that a direct personal approach to the rulers would induce many of them to accept them. His plan was to send his own personal emissaries to the various states to clear the rulers' doubts so that they could make a final decision without delay.[106] The emissaries he chose were Sir Courtenay Latimer, Sir Francis

---

102. Ibid. p.243.
103. *White Paper on Indian States*, p.26.
104. S.R. Mehrotra, op. cit. p.243.
105. He had been the president of the Royal Commission on Agriculture which reported in 1928. On the basis of this report the Imperial Council of Agricultural Research was set up for India. Linlithgow also presided over the Joint Committee of both the Houses of Parliament which examined the White Paper published in March 1933.
106. Foreign and Political Department, no. 20, Federation Secret, 1911.

Wylie and Sir Arthur Lothean all of whom belonged to the Political Service.[107]

The emissaries reported to the Viceroy that the rulers appeared to envisage a federation less organic than that embodied in the Government of India Act.[108] The rulers made it clear that in their case the urge to unity was not dominant, nor were they suppliants asking to come in. The question that agitated them was not whether the federation would enable them to contribute to the benefit of India as a whole, but whether their position would be better and safer inside the federation than outside it. In effect, their attitude could be briefly summed up thus : "We are being given the opportunity of entering a federation from which, when once we are in, there is no escape. Nor since the ultimate interpreter of the federal constitution is the Federal Court, can the Government of India or anyone else predict the course of future events or anticipate the use which federation will make of its powers. We own it therefore to ourselves and to our successors to safeguard to the utmost our own position inside the federation. This is the light in which you must regard the limitations which we have proposed, and if they seem unduly numerous and too widely drawn, remember that we have good reasons for making them so."[109]

The limitations proposed by the rulers could be traced mainly to a desire to safeguard two things : first, their sovereignty and secondly, their financial position; and although the relative importance assigned to one or the other varied from state to state both were regarded as vital by the states as a whole.

In may 1937 the Secretary of State (the Marquess of Zetland) had informal talks with a number of rulers and Indian

---

107. Ibid. no. 353, Federation Secret, 1936.
108. V.P. Menon, op. cit. p.36-
109. Ibid. p.37.

politicians who happened to be in England. It was his impression that the rulers generally were unwilling to accept the federation and that the viceroy was dealing with unwilling takers.

An informal conference of the rulers was held in October 1936 to discuss the Act of 1935 as a whole, and it was decided to appoint a committee of the princes and ministers to examine the provisions of the Government of India Act from the point of view of the states' entry into the federation.[110] It was to report its findings to the standing committee by the end of 1937.

The committee's report suggested certain limitations on various federal items. It also suggested that the question of the scope of paramountcy should be taken up in a not too distant future.[111] It criticised the dual personality of the Governor-General as the representative of the Crown as well as the Head of British India and expressed its apprehension that "federal responsibility might engross the greater part of his time and the distinction between his two personalities might be blurred in which the federal personality would also certainly become dominant."[112]

Thus, until 1938, the federation scheme remained stagnant : very little progress was achieved in the negotiations with the rulers. It was evident that the princes' demands could not be acceptable unless and until the basic principle of the federation was renounced. The safeguards demanded by the states were such that they could not possibly be accepted in a federal scheme.

---

110. *Report of the Constitutional Committee of the Chamber of Princes*, Hindustan Times Press, Delhi, pp. 9-10.

111. *Report of the Constitutional Cammittee*, pp.21-40.

112. Foreign and Political Department no.1, Federal Internal (Secret), 1937.

The viceroy at last decided to confront the rulers with the final offer. Accordingly in January 1939, he addressed a circular letter to the rulers of all the salute states, enclosing the revised draft of the Instrument of Accession along with the schedules and the draft acceptance of the crown.[113] The letter emphasized that there was no prospect of any substantial variation of the term indicated in the direction of following a lesser measure of accession than that which was shown therein, or of modifying or adding to the limitations specified.

The reply came sooner than was expected. At a second conference of rulers and states' minister held in Bombay, the following resolution was passed : "The Conference of Princes and Ministers assembled at Bombay, having considered the revised draft of the instrument of accession and connected papers resolve that the terms on the basis of which accession is offered are fundamentally unsatisfactory in the directions indicated in the report of the Hydari Committee of Ministers and confirmed by the recommendations of the Gwalior Conference and are therefore unacceptable. At the same time, the conference records its belief that it could not be the intention of His Majesty's Government to close the door on all India federation."[114]

The princes also prepared an aide-memoire in which satisfactory adjustment on some of the essential issues in the terms of accession was demanded. Reviewing the aide-memoire, the viceroy clarified certain points with regard to the Instrument of Accession and refuted the allegations of some of the princes that pressure was being put upon the princes to join the federation.

However, the outbreak of the Second World War in September 1939 made the British Government announce the

---

113. Foreign and Political Department, Federation Secret, 1939.

114. V.P. Menon, op. cit. p. 37.

suspension of the negotiations and the establishment of the contemplated federation remained a distant goal.

Some observers blamed the viceroys, Willingdon[115] and Linlithgow for not pressing ahead with the scheme of federation speedily enough. They regretted that the Second World War intervened and the federal proposals had to be shelved. They also asserted that if the federation materialized by 1939 the partition of India, with all the turmoil and bloodshed and other ramifications would have been avoided.[116]

To the princes much of the essence of the federation appeared to turn out to be the negation of all to which they had been accustomed. Their approach to the problem was constrained by the view that their accession to the federation involved a process of levelling down so far as their internal sovereignty was concerned as against the provinces which were to be levelled up as autonomous units and that, therefore, the provinces and states could not be treated alike.[117] On the other hand, progressive public opinion in British India hardened against the apparent effort of the princes to whittle down the content of their accession to a farce no less than against such reactionary features of the federal scheme as the installation of dyarchy at the centre in the form of the reserved subjects in the hands of the Governor-General, i.e., Defence and External Affairs. Meanwhile, the Muslim League veered round to a position of determined hostility to all the constitutional plans which envisaged a common centre for the whole of India. Finally the reactionary elements had their sway and the federation scheme of 1935 proved still-born.[118]

---

115. Willingdon had adopted a dual policy : even as he carried on measures for constitutional reform sketched out by the British government he tried to suppress the Civil Disobedience Movement, jailed Gandhi in January 1932 and proscribed the Congress.
116. Mehrotra, op. cit. p. 243.
117. *White Paper on Indian States*, p. 26.
118. Ibid.

S.R. Mehrotra, in one of his articles, says that the failure of the scheme of federation should not be regretted. According to him, the princes were not wise enough at this juncture and were ultimately swept sway. It would have been a disaster if they had seen their way to join in the making of an Indian federation in the late 1930s. A federation which included some states and excluded other states, which enjoyed different powers and fuuctions in different states, was unlikely to promote Indian unity. If the integrity, sovereignty and autonomy of the Indian states had been recognised and institutionalized by some federation in the 1930s it would have been impossible to revise the process in 1947.[119]

After the Congress ministries came into power the major provinces in 1937, the congress policy of non-involvement in states' politics rapidly gave place to a more 'activist policy'—"a policy of undisguised hostility to the states' governments and of open encouragement of agitation within and without the states against them."[120] In the face of the popular agitation going on in many states during 1938-39, it was difficult to expect the princes to be prepared to associate themselves closely with the political leaders of British India who, they thought, were the root cause of the agitation. This was made amply clear by the Jam Sahib of Nawanagar who maintained that the political situation and the hostility in British India towards the states "proved a decisive factor with many princes."[121]

119. S.R. Mehortra, op. cit. p. 243.

120. R. Coupland, *Indian Politics*, 1936-42, p. 5.

121. *Proceedings of the Chamber of Princes*, 1940, no. 48, p. 42.

4

The States' Peoples' Movement at its Height

The years following the introduction the 1935 Act were most significantly marked by the spread of nationalist movement in the princely states—the bulwarks of autocracy and rampant feudal exploitation which British Federation plans had increasingly exposed as key supporters of imperialism, trying to keep India divided and subjugated. The initiative for the movement came from below : The All India States' Peoples' Conference was active under its Secretary Balwant Rai Mehta. The uprisings which took place, showed the consciousness as well as the determination of the states peoples to get their grievances redressed. Some rulers took stern measures to suppress the agitation, forcing their subjects to seek help from British Indian politicians. The Congress which had all along maintained its policy of 'benevolent neutrality' towards the states now felt inclined to revise its policy[1].

The implementation of the provincial part of the Government of India Act of 1935 and the overwhelming

---

1. N.N. Mitra, *The Indian Annual Register*, vol. I, 1938, p. 41.

success of the Congress in the elections to the provincial legislatures in 1937 encouraged the states' subjects to agitate for civil liberties and responsible government.[2] During theyears 1935-39 the All India States' Peoples' Conference strengthened itself by forming local organizations. Several regional States Peoples organisations such as the Orissa States' Peoples' Conference and the Deccan State's Peoples' Conference were formed After the initial success of the Bijolia Peasant Movement the Mewar Praja Mandal was formed in April 1938. Others like Kathiawar State's Peoples' Conference and Travancore Political Conference held their sessions and discussed the various burning issues affecting them.[3] At the same time, they intensified its activities by publicising the States' Peoples' cause. The All India States' Peoples' Conference published many books and pamphlets such as the Orissa States Enquiry Committee Report, "Bikaner", "Ratlam", and "Jhabua". The incarceration in the jails of some of the states in connection with the Civil Disobedience Movement brought the states' workers into contact with the leaders of British India and provided them with better political understanding and insight.[4] Now greater political maturity became evident from the pronouncements of the All India States' Peoples' Conference and in the action of its political workers. In the fifth session held at Karachi in July 1936, it decided its creed as the attainment for the people of the states a fully "democratic responsible government by all peaceful and legitimate means."[5]

There was unrest in Mysore, Travancore, Kashmir, Hyderabad, Jaipur, Rajkot and other Orissa states, to name only a few. There were peoples' movements exhibiting the sentiments of sub-nationalism. Even though some of these

---

2. V.P. Menon, op. cit. p. 42.
3. *The State's People*, vol. I, no. 5, February 1939.
4. N.D. Parikh, *Sardar Vallabhbhai Patel*, vol. II, p. 295.
5. Pattabhi Sitaramayya, Presidential Address, AISPC, Karachi, 1936.

movements lacked broad civic outlook, and suffered from immaturity and want of competent leadership, many of them were the outcome of the new political awakening and were rooted in certain genuine grievances as well as aspirations of the people. They were both political and economic in character. Besides demanding freedom of association and speech, and constitutional reforms such as the establishment of elected legislatures, constitutional governments and the rule of law, they also pressed for the redress of their economic grievances and relief from the political highhandedness of their rulers.[6]

The main demands of the National Conference of Kashmir were the grant of responsible government, an elected legislature, special safeguards to the minorities in all spheres; equal opportunity of employment to all without any discrimination of race, class or caste; freedom of life, liberty and property, or association and speech etc.[7] In Hyderabad, the demands of the people were : the lifting of the ban on the Hyderabad State Congress ; immediate release of the political prisoners ; the grant of fundamental rights to the people ; the establishment of an elected government ; the decommunalisation of services ; compulsory primary education ; and discontinuance of the Princes' Protection Act.[8] Rajkot Praja Parishad demanded the abolition of monopoly in matches, and cinema, among other things.[9] Mansa demanded a reduction in the land revenue.

Though in certain cases the movement was confined to certain urban sections of the people, in others it was essentially agrarian in character, based, as it was on the peasants'

---

6. Urmila Phadnavis, op. cit. p. 116.
7. "Events in Kashmir", *The States People*, vol. I, no. 1, Oct. 1938, 6 A and B.
8. "The Cry for Freedom", ibid. no. 3, December 1938.
9. "Rajkot Makes History" *The States People*, vol. I, no. 2, November 1936.

economic demands such as the reduction of land revenue and rent, and manned by village folk in larger numbers.[10]

In some cases the movement was led by the local people who had hardly any political experience, although in others it was led by those who had participated in the Civil Disobedience Movement and were inspired by the Gandhian spirit. While some of them could claim the able leadership of Sardar Vallabhbhai Patel, one of the topmost leader of the Congress, and of Seth Jamnalal Bajaj, in others leaders like Mahatma Gandhi, Jawaharlal Nehru, another topranking leader, and B. Kripalani[11] intervened when the occasion demanded.

The political movements in the states did command the moral support and sympathy of the Congress established in 1937 in many provinces, but they did not extend them any active support.

Popular movements had different manifestations in different states. Similarly, the reactions of the princes to these movements varied. In October 1937 the All-India Congress Committee meeting at Calcutta, censured the Mysore Government in the strongest terms for its policy of repression and appealed to the people of the Indian states and British India 'to give all support and encouragement to the people of Mysore in the struggle against the state for the right of self-determination.'[12] Gandhi was not happy over this resolution and criticised it in the column of the *Harijan* as going against the Congress creed of non-interference in the affairs of the states.[13] Gandhi's view was welcomed by the government circles.

10. N.D. Parikh, op. cit. vol. II, p. 372.
11. Kripalani born in 1888, was the General Secretary of the Congress (1934-45).
12. *Indian National Congress Resolutions*, 1936-38, pp. 19-20.
13. M.K. Gandhi "The AICC", *Harijan*, vol. V, no. 59, November 13, 1937, p. 332.

But soon he had to change his stance. In January 1938, he threatened to make an incident in Jaipur an all-India issue when Jamnalal Bajaj, one of his close associates, was arrested there. Gandhi declared that the Congress would be neglecting its duty if it allowed the spirit of the people to be crushed for want of support from the Congress.[14]

In February 1938, at the Haripura session of the Congress, a fuller though more moderately worded resolution, was passed, explaining the Congress policy towards the states. The Congress reiterated its objective of standing for the same political, social and economic freedom in the states as in the case of the rest of India, and of considering the states as the integral parts of India.[15] It declared for the first time *Purna Swaraj* ideal to cover the states as much as British India.[16] The Congress, the resolution continued, was not yet able to obtain the liberation of the states' subjects by itself operating within their borders. In the existing conditions, "the burden of carrying on the struggle for freedom must fall on the people of the States."[17] Only false hope would be raised if they relief on extraneous help or assistance or on the prestige of the Congress name. The Congress as an organization could only offer moral support and sympathy. But individual congressmen would be free to render further assistance in their individual capacities, but the Congress committee which had come into existence in the states "must submit to the control of the working committee and must not engage in politics under the Congress name."[18]

The resolution was intended to soft-pedal the agitation in the states. But it was not easy even for Gandhi to draw a 'khadi curtain' screening the states from the general mass

---

14. V.P. Menon, op. cit. p. 43.
15. *Indian National Congress Resolution*, 1938-39, no. 51, pp. 10-12.
16. Ibid.
17. Ibid.
18. Ibid.

awakening.[19] A radical left-wing had by this time developed within the Congress pleading for a revolutionary policy with regard to the states. No wonder individual congressmen started leading the agitations in some states. The Congress ministries of the provinces adjoining some states declined to use their statutory powers to prevent agitation being organized within their provinces and launched beyond them. The situation was compared to the form of 'non-intervention' practised in the civil war in Spain.[20]

Gandhi's attitude towards the states gradually changed much. In an article in the *Harijan* in December 1938, he acclaimed the simultaneous awakening in the states as due to the 'time spirit' and found it impossible "to defend it in the face of injustice perpetrated in the states." If the Congress felt that it had the power to offer effective interference, "it will be bound to do so when the call comes."[21] He further declared that there was no half-way house between total extinction of the states and full responsible government.[22]

In an interview with the press correspondent of the *Times of India*, Gandhi maintained that "the policy of non-intervention by the Congress was, in my opinion, a perfect piece of statesmanship when the people of the states were not awakened. That policy would by cowardice when there is all round awakening among the people of the states and a determination to go through a long course of suffering for the vindication of their just rights. If once this is recognised, the struggle for liberty, whenever it takes place, is the struggle for all India. When the Congress thinks it can usefully intervene, it must intervene.[23]

---

19. V.P. Menon, op. cit. p. 43.
20. Ibid.
21. Gandhi, *The Indian States' Problem*, p. 104.
22. Ibid. p. 101.
23. *Times of India*, Bombay, 25 January 1939.

Referring to a rumour that the British Government would go back on a statement made by Lord Winterton in Parliament about the right of the rulers to grant responsible government to their people, he thought that any such recantation would precipitate a first class crisis "whose magnitude it is difficult to foretell."[24] Alluding to the excesses committed by the states' police in suppressing agitation, he claimed that the provincial ministers had the moral right and duty to take notice of gross misrule in the states, and to advise the paramount power on what should be done. He then gave a warning that the Congress policy of non-interference might be abandoned; and he advised the rulers to cultivate friendly relations "with an organization which bids fair in the future, not very distant, to replace the paramount power—led me hope, by friendly arrangement."[25]

The States' Peoples' Movement figured prominently at Tripuri (near Jabalpur) session of the Congress during March 1939. In his presidential address, Subhas Chandra Bose praised the "unprecedented awakening" of the people in the states and asserted that the Congress should revise its attitude towards the states as defined by the Haripura Congress resolution. Since Haripura much had happened and therefore "should we of Congress not draw closer to the people of the states?"[26] At the same session, Mrs. Kamala Devi Chattopadhyaya, added that, to elicit correct information as to what was going on in the states, a better co-ordination of the Congress with the All India States' Peoples' Conference was necessary.[27]

The Congress, in its resolution, expressed sympathy with the states' peoples and advised the princes to march with the times. The policy of non-intervention was "dictated by circums

---

24. V.P. Menon, op. cit. p. 43.
25. Ibid. p. 44.
26. *Report of the Second Session of the Indian National Congress*, Tripuri, Mahakoshal, 1939, pp. 65-6.
27. Ibid. p. 179.

tances and by a recognition of the limitations inherent in the circumstances, but it was never conceived as an obligation."[28] The Congress, claimed the resolution, "has always possessed the right, as it is its duty, to guide the people of the states and lend them its influence. The great awakening that is taking place among the people of the states may lead to a relaxation or to a complete removal of the restraint which the Congress imposed upon itself, thus resulting in an over-increasing identification of the Congress with the States' People."[29]

The resolution reiterated its demand of complete independence for the whole of India inclusive of the states. It was decided that the Congress committee, would meet the Standing Committee of the All India States' Peoples' Conference to devise ways and means of bringing about closer co-operation among the people of the Indian states and British India. Thus the Tripuri resolution bridged the gulf between the Indian National Congress and the All India States' Peoples' Conference and led to a gradual identification of the two bodies.[30]

The princes of different states reacted to this new political awakening in the states in different ways. The local Prajamandal had started agitation in Rajkot for political and administrative reforms under U.N. Dhebar.[31] Virawala, the very unpopular Dewan of Rajkot, had imposed numerous

---

28. *INC Resolution*, March 1939 to January 1940, no. 51 p. 7.
29. Ibid.
30. Phadnavis, op. cit. p. 128.
31. "Rajkot makes History", *The States People*, vol. I, no. 2, November 1936. Uchharangray Navalshankar Dhebar, born in 1905, gave up his legal practice in 1936 and started the work of village-uplift. He organised the Rajkot Mill Kamagar Mazdoor Sangh in the teeth of the opposition of the Diwan of Rajkot. He also revived the Kathiawad Political Conference after eight years of inactivity and got Sardar Patel and Darbar Gopaldas to address its session. He was arrested by the Rajkot darbar in 1937 : S.P. Sen (ed.), op. cit. vol. I, p. 455.

monopolies disliked by the local traders and stopped summoning an advisory elected council set up earlier. while nearly half the revenues of the state were swallowed by the privy purse of its ruler. Gandhi together with Sardar Patel intervened in the Rajkot affair. In the famous Rajkot *satyagraha* in 1938-39. Kasturba Gandhi and Maniben Patel courted arrest in Feburary 1939, and Gandhi himself started a fast in Rajkot on the eve of the Tripuri Congress. Then Patel intervened and a compromise was effected between the Thakur of Rajkot and his subjects. But soon the British Political Department instigated Virawala to withdraw the concessions he had offered earlier.[32]

Linlithgow wrote to the Secretary of State, "It was of vital importance that the State [Rajkot] should not allow itself to be rushed and that while ensuring that any action necessary to remedy short-comings and grievances was taken, it should resist any endeavour on the part of the Congress to come in as arbitrators or the like." He had little doubt that "if Congress were to win in Rajkot case the movement would go right through Kathiawad and they would then extend their activities in other directions."[33]

Meanwhile for more impressive and significant movements had started in many other parts of princely India, most notably in Mysore in the south, the Orissan states in the north-east, Hyderabad and Trawancore as well as in parts of Rajputana and the Punjab States of Patiala, Kalasia, Kapurthala and Sirmoor.

Gandhian influence remained fairly firm in Mysore where K.T. Bhasyam's State Congress initially based on Brahman urban professional groups, extended its support through merger in October 1937 with the Peoples Federation of non-Brahman rural landholders led by K.C. Reddy and H.C. Dasappa.[34] A first round of agitation from October 1937

---

32. Ibid.
33. Tarachand, *History of Freedom Movement in India*, vol. IV, p. 261.
34. Sumit Sarkar, *Modern India*, 1885-1947, p. 367.

for the legalization of the Congress as well as for a responsible government culminated on 11 April 1938 in a bloodbath at Viduraswathi village in the Kolar district where 30 agitationists were killed by a firing on a crowd of 10,000. In the following month Patel concluded a truce with Dewan Mirza Ismail which legalized the Congress, but the failure to implement the promises of significant constitutional reform led to another round of civil disobedience from September 1939.[35]

In Aundh, the ruler, almost of him own accord, granted to his people constitutional reforms of far-reaching character, and decided to devote the resources of his state to the promotion of their welfare.[36] Baroda, without much difficulty, consented to reduce the land revenue even though it meant reduction in the state's resources by 20 lakhs.[37] Mansa followed Baroda in reducing the assessment. The State also recognised peasants' proprietary rights in land.[38] Jaipur had the audacity to ban the Praja Mandal and the entry of Seth Jamnalal Bajaj into Jaipur but ultimately consented to lift the ban and to withdraw regulations regarding public meetings. He also assured people's amelioration in certain directions.[39]

But the rulers of many states of Saurashtra, Orissa, Central India and Rajasthan such as Limbdi,[40] Dhenkanal,[41]

---

35. Parikh, op. cit., no. 4, pp. 303-4.
36. 'Constitution for Aundh', *The States People*, vol. I, no. 1.
'Aundh leads the way', ibid., vol. 1, no. 5, February 1939, pp.22-3.
37. Parikh, op. cit., no. 4, pp. 371-2.
38. Ibid., pp. 307-8.
39. Anand T. Hingorani, *To the Princes and the People*, Karachi, 1942, pp. 253-289.
40. Parikh, op. cit.; no. 4, pp. 374-84.
41. Sarangdhar Das, 'Lathi to Manufacture Loyalty : Military Zoolum in Dhenkenal'. *The States People*. vol. I, no. 2, November 1938, p. 5.

Talcher,[42] Nilgiri,[43] Ratlam,[44] Jhabera,[45] Jodhpur[46] and Udaipur[47] were determined to crush the political unrest ruthlessly at all costs. They initiated a reign of terror in their respective states and some even preferred devastation and depopulation to political concession. Perhaps Limbdi surpassed others in repressive methods. To undermine the political movement of the Praja Mandal, the state not only encouraged Hindu and Muslim citizens to organise communal organisations such as Sanatan Mandals and Muslim Jamait, but also instigated the village officers and certain mischievous elements to use coercion against the workers and sympathisers of Praja Mandal who were brutally assaulted and robbed of their property with impunity. All this organised violence and gangsterism were carried out principally by or at the instigation of persons who were either in the service of the state or its dependents. Even the conference of Praja Mandal, scheduled to be held on 19 February 1938, was disrupted by the "mischievous elements." The people were so terror striken that 6,000 out of a total population of 41,000 migrated to the adjoining districts of British India.[48] In Talchuabe, due to the serious acts of tyranny, 26,000 persons out of a total population of 75,000 emigrated to other areas.[49]

In the biggest princely state Hyderabad, a small Muslim elite held ninety per cent of the government jobs, and Urdu

---

42. Parikh, op. cit., no. 4, p. 298.
43. Akshay Kumar Desai, *Indian Feudal States and National Liberation Struggle*, p. 48.
44. Ratlam, *A Report submitted to the President of the AISPC*, pp. 35-52.
45. *Jhabua under Council Administration—A True Picture*, K L. Vaidya, Bombay, 1936, pp. 1-30 and *Struggle of Jhabua State's Subjects* : An Appeal to Paramount Power, K.L. Vaidya, Bombay, 1936, p. 16.
46. 'The Fear of Rajputana', *The States People*, vol. I, no. 2, 1938, p. 4.
47. *The States People*, vol. I, no. 2 and nos. 13-14.
48. *Lawless Limbdi*, AISPC, Bombay, pp. 1-88.
49. Parikh, op. cit.,. no 4, p. 298.

was maintained as the sole official language and the medium of instruction in a state which was fifty per cent Telgu, twenty-five per cent Marathi and eleven per cent Kannada speaking. There was a total absence of elementary civil and political rights, and extremely crude forms of feudal exploitation like forced labour and compulsory payments in kind, prevailed in the Telangana region. Popular awakening initially took the form of middle class language-based cultural associations—the Andhra Mahasabha in Telangana and Maharashtra Parishad in Marathwada—petitioning for political reforms.[50] At about the same time, a State Congress had been founded on a secular basis by Swami Ramananda Tirtha and Govinddas Shroff from Marathwada, Ravi Narayan Reddi from Telangana and a few Muslims like Sirajul Hassan Tirmiji from Hyderabad city. A powerful 'Vandemataram' movement developed among Osmania university students, who left their institutions when the Nizam banned the singing of that patriotic song. Despite the secular frame of the Hyderabad State Congress the Nizam of Hyderabad banned it in September 1938 on the plea that it was "constituted on communal lines."[51] The Congress activities, however, were withdrawn at Gandhi's insistence in December 1938, ostensibly on the ground that it could get mixed up with the Hindu communalist agitation. Ramananda Tirtha was taken aback and said, "We could not understand the propriety of this decision."[52] Soon 'the cream of Andhra workers who had given the lead under Ravi Narayan Raddy joined the communist ranks.[53]

In Travancore and Cochin, as in the adjoining Malyali district of Malabar, the national movement was built up very

---

50 Sumit Sarkar, *Modern India*, p. 368.

51. *The Struggle for Freedom in Hyderabad State*, Hyderabad State Congress. Bombay, 1938, pp. 10-30. Vande (Bande) Mataram means Hail (salute) Motherland.

52. Tirtha, Ramananda, *Memoirs of Hyderabad Freedom Struggle*, Bombay, 1967, p. 107.

53. Ibid., p. 87.

largely under leftist leadership and guidance. In August 1938, the Travancore State Congress started a powerful agitation against the Dewan C.P. Ramaswami Aiyer. Despite brutal repression, the students joined the *Satyagraha* in large numbers, and *jathas* marched into Travancore from many parts of Kerala. The Alleppy coir workers led by Krishna Pillai went on strike in October 1938. The Dewan was forced to call off repressive measures. He also accused the state Congress of communalism,[54] and maintained that the popular movement was the work of the Christians against the Hindu prince.[55]

In Kashmir, popular agitation had already begun under the leadership of the Muslim Conference. On the advice of Jawaharlal Nehru the Muslim Conference of Kashmir was converted into the National Conference. It included as its members many prominent Hindu and Sikh leaders like Jailal Kilam, Sardar Budh Singh, Kashyap Bandhu and P.N. Bazaz.[56] Instead of responding to the anti-autocratic and anti-feudal wishes and aspirations of the people, the Dewan of Kashmir maintained that the States' Peoples' organization was promoted by the Muslims against the Hindu prince.

Some of the bigger and middle sized states, envisaging the intensity of the growing popular agitation, decided to meet together in order to review the situation and seek the moral and material support of the Paramount Power. With this end in view, the Chief Ministers of many states including Hyderabad, Kolhapur, Travancore, Baroda and Gwalior organised a

---

54. G. Ramchandran, "The Travancore Tragedy", *The States People*, vol. II, no. 13 (4), October-November 1939, pp. 11-12.

55. "Sates' Peoples' Conference Working Committee Resolutions", *The States People*, vol. I, no. 5, December 1938, p. 9.

56. "Valley of Flowers Into Valley of Tears : Struggle for Freedom inKashmir", *The States People*, vol. I, no. 5, Feb. 1939, pp. 27-34.

conference in 1938.[57] The Ministers' Conference decided there that they should send a memorandum to the Political Department with regard to the Congress attitude towards the popular agitation in the states and seek its support, material and moral.[58]

A memorandum was accordingly drafted and sent to the Political Department, declaring that the popular agitation in the states was not an expression of the reaction against the suppressive measures but a drive started by the Indian National Congress "against the Indian States in furtherance of their programme to capture power in the forthcoming Federation."[59] It branded the popular agitation as "a concerted policy" of the Congress "amounting to frantal attack". It also attributed the enhanced strength of the agitation to the statement of Lord Wintertan's statement of February 1938[60] and also to the pronouncements of Lord Lothian, and Lord Samuel, not to mention extreme politicians like Sir Stafford Cripps.[61] It maintained that, if the Government of India announced that "it is not the intention of the paramount power to insist on the grant of partial or complete responsible government or to fetter the choice of the states' representatives to the Federal Legislature as the condition precedent to or as a sine qua non of federation", the agitation would loose its all-India character.[62] The memorandum also asked for moral and material support of the British Government to combat the agitations.[63]

---

57. Foreign and Political Department, no. 647, Political Secret, 1938, N.A.I.
58. Ibid. p. 13.
59. Ibid.
60. Parliamentary Debates, House of Commons, 1937-38, vol. 332, 21 February and 11 March 1938, col. 4.
61. Foreign and Political Department, no. 647, Political Secret, 1938, N.A.I.
62. Ibid., p. 17.
63. Ibid., p. 18.

The British Resident in Kolhapur, Col. Evans Gordon in a letter to the Political Department made a scathing attack on the memorandum. He maintained that such an announcement by the British Government would be "undesirable" as it might be taken by the Congress as a "challenge" and interpreted by the princes as immunity from obligations with respect to constitutional reforms.[64] As regards the princes' request for moral and material support of the British Government, Gordan held that, if the rulers could ask for support to resist "unjustifiable demands", the states' subjects as well had the claim to protection if the attitude of the states towards the subjects could be "held to be unjustified."[65]

In reply to a question in the British parliament on 16 December 1938, the Under-Secretary of State for India declared that it would rest with the rulers to decide what form of government they should adopt. The obligations of the paramount power. he maintained, would "extend to protecting Rulers against violence and disorder and to advising and assisting Rulers in remedying such legitimate grievances of their subjects as may be found to exist."[66]

Thus, the period 1935-39 witnessed the growth of popular movements in the states which, as the princes feared, were coming more and more under the influence of the Congress leaders. The princes, in an effort to crush the movement, not only drove politically conscious sections of their population into the struggle but also led Mahatma Gandhi and the Congress to associate themselves more and more with the States' Peoples' Struggle. In the course of his presidential address at the annual session of the All India States' Peoples' Conference on 15 February 1936, Jawaharlal Nehru warned the princes either to line themselves with the people or be

---

64. Ibid.
65. Ibid.
66. Parliamentary Debates, House of Commons, 1938-39, vol. 342, 28th November to December 22nd 1938, col. 2352.

ready to face the liquidation of their states. He added, "the Congress and the various Praja Mandals have so far made every effort to induce the Rulers to side with their people and establish responsible government. They must realize that for them not to agree to do so will not stop the coming of freedom to their people....It requires no prophet to say with confidence that the Indian States System is doomed even as the British empire, which has so long protected it, is doomed."[67]

67. Presidential Address of Jawaharlal Nehru at the Annual Session of the AISPC, 15 February 1939.

5

The Indian States and the Second World War

The second world war stirred all the political groups in India. Lord Linlithgow had interviews with the leaders of various political parties in the country to bring about a closer association of India with the prosecution of the war. The fall of Burma and Singapore in early 1942 brought the Japanese to the borders of India and the British Government began to think of measures to enlist the co-operation of different political parties in British India which had so far rejected[1] the British Government's call for support in the war.[2] The princes, however, had already expressed their wholehearted support for the war and had contributed considerably in men, money and materials.[3] The princes were having informal discussions with the heads of Supply, Defence and Industry Departments and also participated in National Defence Council.[4] The people of the states were not wholly with the

---

1. Menon, V.P., op. cit., p. 46.
2. Linlithgow, M., *Speeches and Statements 1936-43*, pp. 199-211.
3. *Proceedings of the Chamber of the Princes*, 1940, no. 4, p. 11.
4. Ibid., 1942, no. 4, p. 39.

princes in their stand.[5] Most of them agreed with the Congress that "if the Princes must make their professions in favour of democracy abroad...their first concern should be the introduction of democracy within their own states in which undeluted autocracy reigns supreme."[6]

It was against this background that on March 11 Churchill announced the decision of the war cabinet to send Sir Stafford Cripps, then Lord Privy Seal, to India with proposals for India's attainment of self-government after the war. Churchill also made it clear, however, that the proposals which Sir Stafford was bringing were 'to be accepted as a whole or rejected as a whole.'

Cripps arrived in India on 22 March and on 29 March presented his proposals at a press conference.[7] The Cripps offer consisted of two parts—a long term and a short term offer. The long term plan postulated that immediately after the cessation of hostilities a constitution making body would be set up to frame the constitution of a new Indian union which would have the full status of a dominion with the power to secede, if it chose, from the British Commonwealth.[8] This body would be elected by an electoral college consisting of the members of the lower houses of the provincial legislatures for which fresh elections would be held. This constitution so framed would be accepted and implemented by the British Government on two conditions : First, any province or provinces not prepared to accept the new constiiution, would be entitled to frame by a similar process a constitution of their own giving them the same full status as the Indian union. The second condition was that a treaty

---

5. "States Peoples and the War for Democracy", *The States People*, vol. 2, nos. 13-14, October-November 1939, p. 4.
6. *The Indian National Congress resolution passed between March 1939 to January 1940.*
7. R. Coupland, *The Cripps Mission*, Oxford University Press, Bombay, 1942, p. 29.
8. Ibid., p. 28.

should be negotiated between the British Government and the constitution-making body to cover all matters arising out of the transfer of responsibility, particularly the protection of racial and religious minorities.[9]

Under the short term offer, it was maintained that, until the new constitution was prepared, all political parties must give their active and effective co-operation in the councils of their country, of the commonwealth and of the United Nations for the defence of India and the prosecution of the world war effort as a whole.[10]

So far as the states were concerned, the Cripps declaration was very brief. It stated "whether or not an individual state elects to adhere to the Constitution, it will be necessary to negotiate a revision of its treaty arrangements so far as this may be required in the new situation."[11] The states were to appoint representatives to the constitution making body in the same proportion to their total population as in the case of the representatives of British India as a whole and with the same powers as British Indian members. The states would be free to adhere or not to the new constitution.[12] The rulers were not associated with the Cripps discussions in the same way as the representatives of British India were. But they were very much doncerned with its long-term proposition and, therefore, sought clarifications regarding their position in the long-term plan. For this purpose, a princes' delegation met Cripps on 2 April 1942.[13] The Jam Saheb of Nawanagar, then chancellor of the Chamber of Princes, the late Maharaja Sir Sadul Singh of Bikaner and Maharaja Sir Yadavendra Singh of Patiala

9. Ibid.
10. Ibid., p. 29.
11. N. Mansergh & E.W.R. Lumby (ed.); *Transfer of Power, 1942-47*, HMSO, London, 1970, vol. I, p. 281.
12. Ibid.
13. Foreign and Political Department, no. 192, Political Secret, 1942.

represented the rulers and the Nawab of Chhatari represented the Nizam. The rulers raised several points for elucidation.[14]

The first point raised was whether in the event of a number of states not finding it feasible to adhere to the Union, such states or groups of states would have the right to form a union of their own with full sovereign status.[15] Regarding this Cripps said that personally he did not see any fundamental difficulty in the suggestion but as that situation had not been considered in connection with the present scheme he was not able to give a definite reply.[16]

Dealing with the question of paramountcy Cripps said that in the case of the states adhering to the union, paramountcy would be "automatically dissolved."[17]

On being asked whether in the case of non-adhering states the crown would continue to retain its obligations towards them and would enforce them through the usual sanctions. Cripps replied that this was so; the crown would retain the means to implement its obligation and there would be no change on the questions of paramountcy and other related matters except with their consent.[18]

Some of the rulers wondered if a state's entire treaties with the British Government would have to be revised irrespective of whether it joined the union or not. Cripps explained that the intention was to revise the treaties only so far as might be required in the new situation.[19]

---

14. V.P. Menon, op. cit., p. 49.
15. Foreign and Political Department, no. 192, Political Secret, 1942.
16. Ibid.
17. Ibid.
18. *Transfer of Power*, op. cit., vol. I, p. 510.
19. Foreign and Political Department, no. 192, Political Secret, 1942.

Cripps advised the princes to establish contacts with political parties of British India so that a final decision on the future constitutional changes might be facilitated.[20] He also recommended the extension of joint co-operative grouping scheme to wider units so that, in the event of there not being one union, the "inconveniences" caused by the multiplicity of them would be lessened.[21]

Sir Stafford emphasized that if the Indian peoples were sufficiently reasonable and broad-minded it should be possible for them all to came into a single union. Otherwise they could have separate unions and suffer the inconveniences involved.

This point was well elucidated in the Correspondence of Hyderabad with His Majesty' Government.[22] In its letter of 20 December 1942, Hyderabad expressed its desire to be a separate unit having no organic connection with the Indian union and having direct treaty relations with the British Government. In reply, the Foreign and Political Department appreciated the "soundness of the argument", but at the same time doubted its practicability because a nonacceding state, surrounded as it would be by the territories fully self-governed, could never have friendly relations with the union. Besides, the treaty relations between the states and the Paramount Power were to be replaced by the agreement between the union and non-acceding states. The crown would be nowhere in the picture and a non-adhering state could hardly expect a liberal treatment from the union.[23] Sir Stafford made it clear that the states should look to the Indian Government and not to the British Government for their future.

---

20. Ibid.
21. Ibid.
22. Foreign and Political Department, no. 376, Political Secret, 1942.
23. Ibid.

The Indian states delegation on 10 April sought an assurance from Cripps that non-adhering states should have the right to form a union of their own.

The Cripps proposals were rejected by both the Congress party and the Muslim League. The Congress, apart from ather points such as defence rejected it on the plea that, first, 90 million of the states' people had no representation in the Cripps proposals,[24] and secondly, the principle of non-accession might lead to the balkanisation of India in many states[25] and, therefore, was "severe blow to the conception of Indian unity."[26]

The Cripps Mission brought home to the rulers the discomforting realization that if the interests of British India and the states came into conflict, the British government would almost certainly let down the states.[27] Also, at about this time Jawaharlal Nehru declared that the treaties with the states must be scrapped. The rulers therefore started devising ways to protect their own position and to get a positive assurance from the British government that they would not be sacrificed on the altar of British Indian interests.[28]

The chancellor of the Chamber of Princes in a letter to the Political Adviser on 1 June 1942 had requested the British government for an authoritative statement that they stood true to and firmly by their treaty obligations to the states and would continue to protect them according to their solemn obligations.[29] In their reply, the Political Department pointed out that the literal interpretation of treaties had long been

---

24. M. Gwyer and A. Appadorai (ed.) *Speeches and Documents on the Indian Constitution, 1921-47*, vol. II, pp. 524-6.
25. D.G. Tendulkar, *Mahatma 1940-45*, vol. VI, p. 96.
26. Maulana Abul Kalam Azad, *India Wins Freedom*, p. 62.
27. V.P. Menon, op. cit., p. 52.
28. Ibid.
29. Foreign and Political Department, no. 376. Political Secret, 1942.

affected by usage and suffrance and must become increasingly related to the manner in which the states adapted themselves to the necessities of the changing times.

In a latter of 15 June 1942, the chancellor complained that Cripps, in his discussions on defence matters, had ignored the states completely. Secondly, according to the Cripps declaration, the provinces were given the option to form a union of their own, but the states were not accorded the same privilege. It treated the states as if the Indian states did not matter.[30] Further, he alleged that Cripps received a British Indian as a representative of the so-called States' Subjects Conference which was an adjunct to the Congress.[31] The chancellor further objected to Sir Stafford's suggestion for establishing an effective machinery in the states for ventilating the legitimate grievances of the people.[32]

The Political Department replied that the British government endorsed Sir Stafford's suggestion primarily in the interest of the rulers themselves. But it was for the latter to devise the precise constitutional machinery best suited to them.[33]

Meanwhile, in April 1943, the viceroy announced the attachment scheme for the adminitrative integration of smaller states. Under this scheme, certain semi-jurisdictional states in Kathiawad and Gujarat were attached to the neighbouring states. Collectively the area covered about 7,000 square miles, with a population of 8 lakhs and an annual revenue of about Rs. 70 lakhs.[34]

---

30. Ibid.
31. Ibid.
32. Ibid.
33. Ibid.
34. Foreign and Political Department, nos. 78 and 214, Political Secret, 1944.

The attachment scheme was opposed vehemently both by the smaller states as well as by the Chamber of Princes. It was condemned as "subversive of the cherished heritage of the Indian people, and gravest concern was expressed over the growing tendency to ignore the correct importance and significance of our treaties, sanads and engagements."[35]

The princes submitted to the viceroy the drafts of the resolutions to be placed before the chamber's session of 1944. One of the resolutions urged that the crown's relationship with the states and the crown's powers in respect of the states could not and should not be transferred to any third party and that the fulfilment of the fundamental obligations arising out of the treaties, engagements and sanads should remain an integral part of the British government's policy.

The Political Department expressed the hope that the princes would not move a resolution on the subject. The Standing Committee of the chamber felt insulted and cheated and threatened to resign. The viceroy, however, assured the princes that there would be no further transfer of the relationship of the crown with the states without their consent. Only then did the Standing Committee withdraw its resignation.[36]

By the end of 1944 events had taken a different shape altogether. It locked as though the victory was only a question of time and the war would soon end. There was intense frustration in the country and a complete lull in political activity. About this time the Nawab of Bhopal was elected Chancellor of the Chamber of Princes. He infused new life into the chamber and forged that body into an effective instrument for developing the rulers into a 'Third Force' in Indian politics. He was an advocate of a loose centre with residuary powers in the states. With such a centre and with the Congress and the

35. Section III (b) 71 of 1946, Patiala Archives Chamber.
36. Section V (d) 436 of 1943-46, Patiala Archives.

Muslim League pitted against each other, he imagined the states would occupy a key position and hold the balance.[37]

Now it became evident that the war-time restrictions and measures to quell the popular movement in British India could not be continued for long after the end of the war. Besides, the All India States' Peoples' Conference was strengthened by its identification with the Congress.[38] This identification was evident by their identical approach to the war issue and also in their statements. Besides, the Congress, in consonance with the advice of Mahatma Gandhi, appointed a sub-committee consisting of Nehru, Bhulabhai Desai, Vallabhbhai Patel and J.B. Kripalani to bring the States' people within the orbit of the Congress organisation. The committee recommended the reservation of seats on the basis of population for the states' representatives in the provincial Congress committee. This was accepted by the Congress.[39]

Some workers of the All India States' Peoples' Conference had also participated in the Quit India Movement of 1942.[40] It was clear that the popular movements in the states and the demands of the people which were bypassed in 1939 would have to be taken seriously by the princes.[41]

In March 1945 Lord Wavell flew to England for consultations with the British cabinet. The princes were aware of the impending realization of full self-government for India. The Maharaja of Bikaner wrote to the Maharaja of Patiala that opinion in England appeared to be "impatient for a real move forward which will assure to India the status and powers of a

---

37. V.P. Menon, op. cit. p. 56.
38. 'States' People and The War for Democracy,' *The States People* vol. 2, nos. 13-14, October-November, 1939, p. 4.
39. *Indian National Congress Resolution, 1940-46*, fns. 45, 66 and 93-94.
40. Ibid. fns. 45, 51.
41. Urmila Phadnavis, op. cit. p. 145.

Dominion."[42] He also added that "the period of inactivity necessitated by the overriding consideration of war."[43] Was coming to an end. During 1930-39, the participation of the princes had been a precedent to the grant of federal responsibility; it might not be so now. Consequently, the situation called for a "reorientation of their policy." A special committee of Rulers and Ministers convened in April-May, 1945 in Bombay examined the question of the political adjustment between the states and British India. In June 1945 a detailed resolution on the subject was adopted.

The resolution reviewed the position of the princes in the new political situation and felt that the Cripps formula and the later developments had already indicated that British India might be a dominion even without the adherence of the states. It further emphasised that the war efforts of the states were not likely to make up the loss in the position which the states once enjoyed. Besides, "The British Government will not be in a position in a Dominion India effectively to fulfil its obligations of defence or to safeguard the non-acceding states against economic strangulation or discrimination by the Dominion Government."[44]

The resolution further maintained that the states should utilise the time when gratitude for the war efforts of the states was still fresh in the mind of the government and there was more inclination than might be found later to support their legitimate claims and aspirations.[45] Finally, it concluded that "for this purpose the states should internally set up their houses in order and externally should align themselves with the forces of progress... and [be] second to none in support of legitimate aspirations of India."[46]

42. Section III (C) 71 of 1946, Patiala Archives.
43. Ibid.
44. Ibid.
45. Ibid.
46. Ibid.

The conference also appointed a constitutional Advisory Committee to prepare the case of the states for use at appropriate places.[47] The first meeting of the committee was held in July 1945 to consider the proposals for an interim government as given in a broadcast of Lord Wavell on 14 June 1945.[48] The committee recommended the setting up of a suitable machinery for regular consultations between the representatives of British India and those of the states with regard to the matters of common concern during the interim period.[49]

In September 1945, the viceroy Lord Wavell, on his return from England, announced the government's determination for the early realization of full self-government for India. The steps envisaged were : the summoning of a constitution-making body; consultations with the representatives of the states and the formation of a new Executive Council having the support of the main political parties.[50]

The princes welcomed the plan and the opportunity to participate in the constitution-making body. The question arose : who should represent the states ? The Congress insisted that only popular representatives could represent them, while an important section when to the length of asserting : "we fought and sacrificed our blood to win power and we mean to hold it. If Congress wants to rob us, if the British should let us down, we will fight."[51]

The princes, further, made it clear that any such constitution would be subject to ratification by the princes and that their existing treaties and *sanads* would not be altered unilaterally without their consent.[52]

---

47. Section III (b) 70 of 1946, Patiala States Archives.
48. V.P. Menon, op. cit. p. 58.
49. Section III (b) 77 of 1946, Patiala State Archives.
50. Gwyer and Appadorai (ed.) op. cit. vol. II, pp. 567-8.
51. Menon, op. cit. p. 59.
52. Chamber Section VII (a) 1 of 1946, Patiala Archives.

It was in this context that the annual session of the Chamber of Princes was held on 17 January 1946 under the presidentship of Lord Wavell. In his address, the viceroy assured them that no changes in their relationship with the crown or the rights guaranteed to them by treaties and engagements would be initiated without their consent. At the same time, he expressed his confidence that the states would take their full part in the proposed constitution-making body. For its part, the Chamber of Princes affirmed that the states fully shared the general desire of the country for the immediate attainment of self-government and their intention to make every possible contribution to it.[53]

The Labour Government had now been in power for eight months and so had ample time to take stock of the Indian situation. It also had the benefit of the views of a British parliamentary delegation which had recently toured the country. In a meeting with this delegation, the chancellor, the Nawab of Bhopal, reiterated that the princes earnestly shared the desire of the country for the immediate attainment of her full stature by India and that they were prepared to do all they could to assist it.[54]

---

53. V.P. Menon, op. cit. p. 59.
54. Chamber Section, vol. VII (a) 1 of 1946, Patiala Archives.

6

The Princes and the Cabinet Mission and Constituent Assembly

The assumption of power by the Labour Government in England, the increasing international complications, the aftermath of the war and the growing realization of the fact that it was impossible to keep under subjection four hundred millions of exasperated people, brought about a change in the British policy towards India.[1] A parliamentary delegation visited India in 1945-46 to gain a first hand knowledge of the political situation in this couutry. On 19 February 1946, the Secretary of State for India, Lord Pethick Lawrence, announced his Government's decision to send a delegation of three Cabinet ministers to India[2]

The Mission, consisting of Lord Pethick Lawrence, Sir Stafford Cripps and A.V. Alexander, arrived in New Delhi on 24 March 1946 to settle with Indian leaders the steps for achieving "early realisation of full self-government in India."

---

1. *White Paper on Indian States*, p. 28.
2. *Transfer of Power*, op. cit. vol. VI, p. 1010.

Speaking in Parliament on 15 March, Prime Minister Attlee refering to the Indian states had expressed the nope that princely India and British India would cooperate with each other. Pethick-Lawrence had said at a press conference that they had come in the hope of enabling Indians to produce, or set up a machinery for producing a constitutional structure for India as a whole.[3]

On his arrival in India, Cripps made it clear that in its negotiations the Mission would adhere to the earlier precedents and would consult only the rulers.[4] A suggestion that the Mission should interview the representatives of the states' subjects was not acceptable either to the Political Department or to the Chancellor of the Chamber of Princes. Nor did the Mission itself pursue the question. This disappointed[5] the All India States' Peoples' Conference, which had all along demanded[6] that the states' peoples' opinion should also be taken into account. Authorised by the Standing Committee of the All India States' Peoples' Conference, Jawaharlal Nehru worte to the Mission, insisting that it should meet the representatives of the All India States' Peoples' Conference. Nehru emphasised that "independence conferred upon India

---

3. Ibid. vol. VII, pp. 2-5.
4. Ibid.
5. Statement made by S. Nijalingappa, President of the Mysore States Congress, *Times of India*, 28 March 1946. Similar sentiment was expressed by South Indian States' Peoples organisation on 31 March, *Hindu*, 2 April 1946. Nijalingappa (boan 1902) worked hard for the unification of Karnataka and became its first Chief Minister in 1956.
6. Jai Narayan Vyas, President of Marwar States' Peoples' conference, *National Herald*, Lucknow, 3 March 1946. The Statement of K.C. Reddy, representative of the AISPC in London. *Amrit Bazar Patrika*, 22 March 1946. Also see V.D. Mathur, 'Growth of States' People's Conference in Udaipur, a paper read at the 13th session of the Rajasthan History Congress, March 1982.

would not be complete unless it applied to states' subjects too."[7]

The Cabinet Mission met (1) the chancellor of the Chamber of Princes, (2) the rulers of Patiala, Bikaner and Nawanagar jointly as representing the middle-sized states, (3) the rulers of Dungarpur and Bilaspur jointly as representing the smaller states and (4) the Nawab of Chhalari (Hyderabad), Sir C. P. Ramaswami Aiyar (Travancore) and Sir Mirza Ismail (Jaipur) individually.

In their talks with the Mission, the members of the Chamber, specially the chancellor, made it clear that the states wished to retain the maximum degree of sovereignty. They desired no interference in their internal affairs by British India. The Chancellor suggested the formation of a Privy Council of the states and British India on the lines contemplated in the Simon Report. He was definite that none of the rulers wanted a constitutional set-up of the kind contemplated in the Government of India Act of 1935. On the other hand, he was in favour of a 'loose federation' at the centre. He said that the general view of the rulers was that if there were to be two states in India, there was no reason why a third India composed of the states should not be recognised. Lastly, he pleaded that paramountcy should not be transferred to an Indian government.

The bigger states like Hyderabad and Travancore also agreed with the Chancellor on the issue and maintained that "during the interim period paramountcy would have to be preserved but the machinery of the Political Department would have to be revised." During this period, paramountcy could be executed through the viceroy chosen by the states and working in conjunction with a committee or Advisory Council selected in consultation with the states.[8] The rulers

7. *Hindu*, 10 April 1946.
8. V.P. Menon, op. cit. pp. 62-63.

of Dungarpur and Bilaspur were divided in their views. While the Maharaja of Dungarpur believed that, except six bigger states, all the states should group themselves into larger units "by pooling sovereignty on a regional and linguistic basis", the Raja of Bilaspur did not agree with the idea of grouping and wanted each state to be sovereign and "to be left to itself to do as it wanted" after paramountcy lapsed.

The Nizam of Hyderabad maintained that if the central government were limited to foreign affairs and defence and if there was communal parity.[9] Hyderabad would find it easier to join the federation. But in the event of the partition of the country, it would be impossible for Hyderabad, for geographical reasons, to join Pakistan or, for ideological reasons, to join India. Hyderabad would, in that case, he said, remain independent. He reiterated Hyderabad's demand for the restoration of the territories ceded to the East India Company and wanted a free outlet to the sea, an "easement" to enable the state to import by rail across the Indian territory the goods received at their own port which he wished to be Goa. Cripps, in his reply, told the Nawab that these were matters for subsequent discussions with British India. Sir Mirza Ismail of Mysore wished an interim central executive to include two representatives of the states, a Muslim and a Hindu, and requested that the British should not leave India without having done something to maintain the position of the ruling families, as he considered that they embodied a valued tradition of Indian culture and civilization.[10]

Broadly, the position taken up by the state representatives was that paramountcy should not be transferred to a successor government, but that it should lapse; that the states should not be forced to join any union or unions; that there should be *prima facie* no objection to the formation of a confederation of states if the rulers so desired; and that there

---

9. Ibid. pp. 63-64.
10. Ibid. p. 64.

should be no interference in their internal affairs by British India.[11]

The Cabinet Mission tried to explain the future policy of the British government with regard to the princes. Lord Pethick-Lawrence said that if British India became independent, paramountcy was bound to lapse; that the British government did not contemplate keeping any troops in India for the maintenance of internal order; and that, therefore, as the crown would be unable to carry out its part of the treaty obligations, the states would naturally in their turn be released from their obligations under those treaties. The Mission felt it necessary to make this position clear to the rulers but they did not propose to emphasize, or, unless it became necessary, even to mention this matter to the representatives of British India because it seemed to them that the position of the states in any conversations with the British Indian representatives might be somewhat weakened by a positive statement to that effect. The idea of confederation, as defined by some of the princes, seemed to Lord Pethick Lawrence a novel as well as "an interesting and apparently feasible suggestion." Cripps, however, doubted its practicability for geographical reasons. The Mission also emphasised the necessity of some sort of arrangement—political, economic and administrative between the princes and British India during the interim period. Lastly, it assured the princes that the states' representatives would be consulted again before the future set up of India was finalised.[12]

The Cabinet Mission met the Nawab of Bhopal again on 9 May 1946, and clarified some of his doubts.[13] On 22 May 1946, the Cabinet Mission issued the memorandum in regard to the states' treaties and paramountcy.

The Mission concluded its discussion with different

---

11. Ibid.
12. Ibid. p. 62.
13. VII (a) 16 of 1946, Patiala State Archives.

parties and announced on 16 May 1946, its plan for the setting up of a constitution-making authority.[14] Referring to the states, the Mission said that it was quite clear that with the attainment of independence by British India, whether within or without the British Commonwealth, the relationship which had hitherto existed between the states and the British crown would no longer be possible. Paramountcy could neither be retained by the British crown nor transferred to the new government. The statement went on to say that the rulers had assumed the Mission that they were ready and willing to co-operate in the new development of India. But the precise form which that co-operation would take must be a matter for negotiation during the building up of the new constitutional structure and it by no means followed that it would be identical for all the states.[15]

Under the proposed plan the states were to retain all the subjects and powers other than those ceded to the union, namely, foreign affairs, defence and communications. In the preliminary stage they were to be represented in the Constituent Assembly by a negotiating committee. In the final Constituent Assembly they were to have appropriate representation, not exceeding 93 seats; the method of selection was to be determined by consultation. After the provincial and group constitutions had been drawn up by the three sections of the Constituent Assembly, the representatives of the sections and of the Indian states would reassemble for the purpose of settling the Union Constitution.[16]

The plan did not deal with the states in detail and its vague provisions regarding the association of the states with the Constituent Assembly caused some difficulty as regards the

---

14. *Papers Relating to the Cabinet Mission to India, 1946*, Government of India Press, Delhi, 1946, pp. 1-7.
15. Ibid. p. 3.
16. Ibid. pp. 4-6.

stage at which they could come in as regular members of the Constituent Assembly.[17]

On 22 May the Cabinet Mission published a 'Memorandum on the States' Treaties and Paramountcy.' The Memorandum affirmed that when a new fully self-governing or independent government or governments came into being in British India the British government's influence with these governments would not be such as to enable them to carry out the obligations of paramountcy; nor did they contemplate the retention of the British troops in India for that purpose. Thus, as a "logical sequence and in view of the desires expressed to them on behalf of the Indian states,"[18] paramountcy would lapse and all the rights surrendered by the states to the paramount power would return to the states. The political arrangement between the crown and the states would be brought to an end. This void would "have to be filled either by the states entering into a federal relationship with the successor government or governments in British India, or failing this, entering into a particular political arrangements with it or them."[19]

On 17 May the Nawab of Bhopal wrote to Lord Wavell, asking for further clarification of certain points in the Cabinet Mission plan. He wished to be sure that the authority of the proposed union government and legislature in respect of defence would not in any way affect the right of the states to maintain their own armed forces. The finances of the union, he demanded, should be limited to specific and agreed sources of revenue and there should be no power to raise taxation by any other means. The existing rights of the states in respect of communications should not be affected. The method and manner of representation of the states in the union legislature should rest with the government of the states or groups of states concerned. Any question raising a major issue in the union legislature specifically affecting the states should be

17. *White Papers on Indian States*, p. 29.
18. *Paper Relating to the Cabinet Mission to India*, p. 31.
19. Ibid. pp. 31-32.

dealt with on the same basis as a major communal issue requiring a majority of states' representatives present and voting in its favour. Furthermore, he wanted an assurance that the states so desiring would be free to form a group or groups amongst themselves on such terms and for such purposes as might be mutually agreed upon. The states should have the right to cell for a reconsideration of the Constitution of the union after an initial period of ten years and at ten year's interval thereafter. The constitution-making body should not discuss or make any recommendation in respect of the form of government in the states or the reigning dynasties.[20]

Lord Wavell, in a "non-committal" reply, said that most of the matters refered to by the Nawab could be solved by mutual consultation with British India. As regards the issue of the selection of states' representatives, the viceroy felt that any categorical pronouncement by the Cabinet Mission in the sense desired would render not easier, but more difficult, that free association between the states and British India which it had been the object of of the Mission to projects.[21]

The Nawab of Bhopal found the viceroy's letter "disappointing" and in his letters dated 2 and 3 June pleaded that the British government should not leave the princes as "a sort of no man's child", without safeguarding their rights and prerogatives in the future set-up of India. Lord Wavell, in his reply, asked the Nawab to discuss the issue with Sir Conrad Corfield, the Political adviser to the Government of India.[22]

Sir Conrad had discussions with the Nawab when he addressed the constitutional Advisory Committee of the Chamber of Princes on 8 June,[23] the Committee of State

---

20. *Transfer of Power*, op. cit. vol. VII, pp. 605-609.
21. Ibid. p. 630.
22. Ibid. p. 777.
23. *Hindu*, 10 June 1946.

Ministers on 9 June and the Standing Committee on 10 June, he stated that the decision regarding the lapse of paramountcy at the end of the interim period placed the states in the best bargaining position possible for the purpose of fitting themselves into the future constitutional structure. He advised the states to set-up of a Negotiating Committee to settle the terms on which they would be prepared to participate in the discussions of the constituent Assembly. Besides, he promised that during the interim period the political Department would assist the states in arranging and pursuing negotiations and in the making of practical plans for grouping and affiliation; that it would continue to protect the states, pursue the revision of existing agreements individual states mainly in the economic sphere, and discuss arrangements for minority administrations after the lapse of paramountcy.[24] He finally suggested that if the rulers would maintain continuous personal touch with their subjects and set up real constitutional monarchy in the units of suitable sizes, they would still have a great part to play in the future of India.

The suggestions made Corfield were accepted by the Standing Committee of the Chamber of Princes in a resolution on 10 June 1946. The resolution expressed the view that the Cabinet Mission plan provided the necessary machinery for the attainment by India of independence, as well as a fair basis for further negotiations.[25] It welcomed the declaration of the Cabinet Mission in regard to paramountcy, but pointed out that certain adjustments for the interim period would be necessary.

The Standing Committee set up a Negotiating Committee and authorized the chancellor to arrange discussions with the corresponding body of the British India Constituent Assembly

---

24. VII (a) 16 of 1946, Patiala Archives, Chamber Section.

25. *Papers Relating to the Cabinet Mission to India*, p. 19.

as contemplated by the Cabinet Mission.[26]

The General Council of the All India States' Peoples' Conference met in Delhi during 8 to 11 June to discuss the Cabinet Mission plan. Nearly 200 delegates from all over India participated. Referring to the "explosive background in the Indian states"[27], Jawaharlal Nehru, in his presidential address, emphasised the need of democratisation of the states to bring them up to a common level with the rest of India.[28] He further maintained that paramountcy should vest in the Union Federal Government.[29]

Nehru deplored the fact that the Cabinet Mission had entirely ignored the states' people in its deliberations. He thought that it was odd to argue that the rulers by themselves should decide the fact of nearly 100 million people.[30] "The states people", continued Nehru, "claim to represent for themselves and they will see to it that they are heard. None else, and certainly not their Rulers, can speak for them."[31]

The General Council of the All India States' Peoples' Conference welcomed the announcement of the princes that they stood for "a free and united India." It, however, regretted the way the states' people had been bypassed and ignored by the Cabinet Mission.

The council suggested that, in the Constituent Assembly, the people's elected representatives and not nominated members

---

26. The Committee consisted of the Nawab of Bhopal, the chancellor, the Maharaja of Patiala, the pro-chancellor, Jam Sahib of Nawanagar, the Maharaja of Dungarpur, Sir Mirza Ismail, Sir Ramaswami Mudaliar, Sir C.P. Ramaswami Aiyer, Sir Sultan Ahmed and Sardar K.M. Pannikar.
    VII (a) 11 of 1946, Patiala Archives, Chamber Section.
27. N.N. Mitra, *The Indian Annual Register*, vol. I, 1946, p. 213.
28. Ibid.
29. Ibid.
30. Ibid. p. 214.
31. Ibid.

should participate. It also suggested that even the Negotiating Committee should include the states' peoples' representatives. For the interim period the General Council suggested the formation of an Advisory Council composed of the rulers, the states' peoples' representatives and the representatives from British India, to discuss the matters of common concern. The council also considered the issue of grouping the states to enable them to form a Federal Union, as well as the question of the absorption of the states in the provinces, so that, at the end, the states as single units or as groups, could form" equal units of the Federal Union with equal rights with the provinces and with a democratic structure approximating to that prevailing in the provinces."[32]

The Standing Committee of the All India States' Peoples' Conference in its meeting of 9-10 June, 9-10 July and 19 September 1946, laid emphasis on the recognition of the States' peoples' right of representation in the Constituent Assembly and also appointed a sub-committee of five members with powers to add two more members to prepare the draft proposals on behalf of the states for the coming constitutional changes in India as a whole.[33] In its September meeting, it also expressed its resentment against the exclusion of the states' peoples' representatives in the negotiating committee.[34]

Soon after the publication of the Cabinet plan, the Congress resolved that the Constituent Assembly could not be formed of two conflicting elements and that the manner of appointing the states' representatives for the Constituent Assembly must approximate, so far as possible, to the method adapted in the provinces. It also expressed its grave concern over the crushing of popular demand by some princes.[35]

---

32. Ibid. p. 216.
33. *Hindu*, 10 June 1946.
34. *Leader*, 21 September 1946.
35. INC : *Resolution*, Allahabad, p. 159.

In a press statement at Ahmedabad on 22 May 1946, Gandhi, referring to the possible repercussions of the lapse of paramountcy, maintained that, if it could not be ended with the establishment of the interim movement, it should be exercised in co-operation with it and purely for the benefit of the states' people. He further said, "The princes, if they are true to their profession, should welcome this popular use of paramountcy so as to accommodate themselves to the sovereignty of the people, envisaged under the new scheme."[36]

Vanaja Rangaswami in her book[37] has tried to prove that the Cabinet Mission plan left its provisions regarding the states vague.[38] It was purposely made 'vague' so as to give the rulers a chance at what the Cabinet Mission hoped would be a fair and just arrangement with the leaders of British India as to their future relationship.[39]

It was the vagueness which contributed much to a sense of insecurity of not only the rulers but also of the states' people. The Cabinet Mission while stipulating that paramountcy would neither be retained nor transferred and the void created by the cessation of paramountcy be filled either by the states entering into a federal relationship[40] with the successor government or governments, or into 'particular relationship', with it or with them. Thus the states' confabulations with British India were to be at two levels, one for the etntry into the Constituent Assembly involving discussions on

---

36. *Tribune*, Lahore 4 June 1946.
37. *The Story of the Integration, A New Interpretation*, New Delhi, 1981, p, 196.
38. *Resolution of the Working Committee of the INC*, 24 May 1946. Also see Gwyer and Appadorai (ed.), op. cit. vol. II, p. 593.
39. See Shiva Rao's note on India, 20 August 1945, Document no. 16, pp. 100-105; N. Mansergh (ed.), *Transfer of Power*, vol. VI, pp. 100-105.
40. *Statement by the Cabinet Mission to India, 16 May 1946, Command Paper 6821*, Maurice Gwyer and Appadorai (ed.), op. cit p. 580.

the number and mode of the selection to the same, and secondly on the relationship with British India—federal or otherwise. The British provisions regarding both these were vague, except in suggesting that it be taken up by negotiating committees of both the parties.[41]

The Princes and the Constituent Assembly

The Constituent Assembly met for the first time on 9 December. It elected Rajendra Prasad as the President. On 21 December it passed a resolution appointing a Negotiating Committee to negotiate with a similar body which already been appointed by the Chamber of Princes to deal with the representation of the states in the Constituent Assembly.

The Nawab of Bhopal thought that in order to play the role of an effective "third power" in the politics of India, the rulers should not join the Constituent Assembly individually and immediately but should join at after they had taken a unanimous decision regarding the conditions precedent to their entry to Constituent Assembly and should join *en bloc* after they had finalised their terms of entry in the Constituent Assembly with British India. He greatly resented the declaration of objectives by the Constituent Assembly which not only proposed the setting up of an Independent Sovereign Republic composed of the Indian states and British India but also maintained that the powers and authority of such a republic were to be derived from the people.[42] He maintained that the Cabinet Mission had made it clear that the states' entry into the Federation was voluntary. But he objected to the proposal of the inclusion of all the territories that formed the Indian states in the proposed union.[43] It was "incorrect", said the

---

41. Vanaja Rangaswami, op. cit. p. 196.
42. *Constituent Assembly Debates*, vol. I, no. 5, 13 December 1946, pp. 60-61.
43. II (b) 48 of 1947, Patiala Archives, Chamber Section.

Nawab, "to assume that the states have no option but to come into the proposed structure."[44] He also objected to the wording of the resolution that all the power of the states was derived from the people and maintained that the resolution had raised certain basic and far-reaching issues relating to the Constituent Assembly under the Cabinet Mission plan.[45] In the Conference of Rulers held in Bombay on 29 January 1947, he got adopted a resolution which laid down the conditions necessary for the princes' participation in the deliberation of the Constituent Assembly.

The resolution maintained that, after the termination of the interim period, paramountcy should revert to the princes, and not to the new government of India. The union government would exercise only such functions as were expressly assigned or delegated to it by the states. The constitution of each state, its territorial integrity and the succession of its reigning dynasty should not be interfered with by the union, nor should the existing boundaries of a state be altered except by its free consent. The Constituent Assembly was not to deal with the questions affecting the internal administration or constitution of the states. While the distribution of the state's quota of seats on the Constituent Assembly was a matter for the states to consider and decide among themselves, the method of seletion of the States' Negotiating Committee and the corresponding committee of British India.[46]

The publication of this resolution provoked a good deal of controversy. Public opinion was considerably agitated over the statement made by some rulers that if the fundamental propositions were not accepted by the Congress, they would

44. Ibid.

45. Ibid.

46. *Documents relating to the Statements by His Majesty's Government on 6 December 1946, 20 February 1947 and 3 June 1947*, Government of India Press, Delhi, 1947, pp. 2-3.

boycott the Constituent Assembly.[47] Among the rulers there was a small group which did not see eye to eye with the resolution passed at Bombay. Sir B.L. Mitter, the Dewan of Baroda, under instructions from his ruler, announced on 8 February that he was negotiating direct with the Negotiating Committee of the Constituent Assembly and that he was not bound by the resolution.[48] Accordingly, Baroda decided to join the Constituent Assembly. As early as 30 July 1946, the Maharaja of Cochin had announced his intention of participating in the Constituent Assembly and sending to it only popular representatives elected by the Legislative Council of the state.[49] Several Rajputana states were also thinking on the same lines. "We cannot afford", declared one leading representative of the states," to create the impression that we intend to sabotage the Constituent Assembly."[50]

The majority of the states still stood by the Negotiating Committee of the Chamber of Princes. This body met the British Indian counterpart for the first time on 8 February. The spokesmen of Constituent Assembly Negotiating Committee replied that it was not concerned with any undertaking given to the princes by the viceroy or by the British government. It was only concerned with the Cabinet Plan.[51] The only function assigned to the Negotiating Committee on both the sides was, first, to determine the method of selecting representatives of Indian states and, secondly, the manner in which the seats assigned to the Indian states should be distributed. The Negotiating Committee, it maintained, had no mandate to discuss the fundamental proposition raised in the resolution of 29 January.[52] Each side adhered to its own point of view and the first joint meeting ended inconclusively.

---

47. V.P. Menon, op. cit. p. 72.
48. Ibid.
49. Ibid. *The Hindu*, 12 January 1947.
50. *The Hindu*, 2 February 1947.
51. VII (a) of 1947, Patiala Archives, Chamber Section.
52. Ibid. VII (a) 11 of 1946.

On 9 January, the Nawab of Bhopal repeated his previous day's stand that his committee was bound under its instructions to secure a satisfactory settlement of the fundamentals. It thus appeared that the deadlock would continue but the Maharaja of Patiala intervened and sought clarification of the previous day's discussions. Speaking on behalf of the Congress, Jawaharlal Nehru said that the meeting was proceeding on the basis of the Cabinet Mission plan. He went on to say that the issue of a monarchical form of government in the states did not arise out of the plan nor the British Indian representatives wish to come in the way of this form of government. The Congress had no idea of changing the states boundaries without the consent of the parties concerned. He added that the scheme under Cabinet Mission plan was a voluntary one and there would be no compulsion at any stage. After this conciliatory statement, the atmosphere became more friendly and the meeting went on to consider the question of filling up the 93 seats allotted to the states.[53] It was decided that a scheme of distribution should be worked out jointly by the secretaries of the Constituent Assembly and of the Chamber of Princes and the meeting adjourned till 1 March 1947.

The confabulations of the negotiating committees make it clear that the Congress, for its part, was anxious to secure the co-operation of the princes in order to improve the chances of success of the Constituent Assembly. The princes, on the other hand, were anxions to retain unity in their ranks and wanted to avoid a state of affairs in which some among them might follow the example of Baroda, thereby entering into direct negotiations with the Congress.[54]

On 20 February 1947, British Prime Minister Attlee made a declaration in the House of Commons in the course of which he set a date not later than June 1948 by which Britain would transfer power to the responsible Indian hands. It was also

53. Ibid.
54. Urmila Phadnavis, op. cit, p. 168.

decided that Viscount Mountbatten of Burma would replace Lord Wavell as viceroy. With regard to the states, the declaration stated : "As was explicitly stated by the Cabinet Mission, His Majesty's Government do not intend to hand over their powers and obligations under paramountcy to any government of British India. It is not intended to bring paramountcy, as a system, to a conclusion earlier than the date of the final transfer of power, but it is contemplated that for the intervening period the relations of the crown with individual states may be adjusted by agreement."[55]

The announcement had diverse effects upon the princes. The states like Hyderabad[56] and Travancore declared that, after the transfer of power, they would be independent. Travancore decided not to participate in any meeting of the Constituent Assembly because it maintained that it would be independent after June 1948, subject to negotiations with the union on matters of common concern.[57] Some princes thought of breaking off their negotiations with the Constiuent Assembly on the plea that the Constituent Assembly was "not fully representative and was not functioning as it was intended under the Cabinet Mission Plan."[58] The Nawab of Bhopal again reiterated this old stand in a memorandum stating that the mandate contained in the resolution of 29 January should be taken as a condition precedent to the states' entry to the Constituent Assembly.

The approach in this memorandum was not acceptable to an influential section of the rulers, and the Maharaja of Bikaner, Sardul Singh, declared his opposition to the policy recommended by the chancellor. He emphasised that "the united front which was required to be put up by the states could not be attained by a policy of 'wait and see' but by co-

55. V.P. Menon, op. cit. p. 73.
56. *The Tribune* (editorial), 2 March 1947.
57. *The Times of India*, April 1947.
58. *The Hindustan Times*, 28 February 1947.

operation with the Constituent Assembly." He added that if the states did not co-operate, it would give an impression that the states were playing into the hands of certain political parties in British India.[59] Such a policy, he held, would give "a loophole to the interested parties to make a mischief in every possible way."[60] He referred in particular to the Muslim League's policy and said that, even if it did not join the constitution-making body, and interests of the states, "inter-personal as they are with territories of India" lay in the creation of a "strong central government" which would fill "vacuum that would be created by the withdrawal of the British Government." The only safe policy for the states, therefore, was to work fully with the stabilizing elements in British India to create a centre for taking over from the British.[61] The interest of the people of the states obviously lie in joining hands with British India in establishing a strong centre. And they are keenly alive to that necessity. But if for any reason, the princes were to decide otherwise, they would be putting themselves in opposition to the very strong wishes and interests of their people.

The Maharaja of Bikaner's lead was followed by the Maharaja of Patiala, who also issued a public statement depreclating the policy of 'sitting on the fence'.[62]

The Maharaja of Bikaner declared that in view of the basic differences with his colleagues, he would not participate in the meeting of the Standing Committee.[63] Thus the Patiala-Bikaner group had finally made up its mind to join the Constituent Assembly.

---

59. V.P. Menon, op. cit. p. 75.
60. VII (a) 17 of 1947 (Confidential), Patiala Archives, Chamber Section.
61. V.P. Menon, op. cit. p. 75.
62. Ibid. pp. 75-76.
63. 17 of 1947 (Confidential), Patiala Archives, Chamber Section.

The firm stand taken by the Bikaner-Patiala group had its effect on the general conference of the rulers and the states' ministers which met on 2 April 1947. As a result, the original draft resolution was watered down and another adopted in its place. By this resolution, the conference reiterated the willingness of the states to render the fullest possible co-operation in framing an agreed constitution and towards facilitating the transfer of power on an agreed basis. A resolution embodying the formula permitted freedom to the member states of the chamber to enter the Assembly at any stage they might deem fit after the Assembly had ratified the Agreement between the negotiating committee of the chamber and of the Assembly.[64]

The Nawab of Bhopal still tried to dissuade the rulers from entering the Constituent Assembly but did not succeed, and on 29 April 1947, the representatives of the states of Baroda, Bikaner, Patiala, Cochin, Jaipur and Rewa took their seats in the Assembly.[65] Subsequently, with the exception of Hyderabad, all the remaining states entitled to individual representation also sent their representatives to the Constituent Assembly of India. Representatives were also returned in due course by a group consisting of the states which did not have individual representation.[66]

It is remarkable that the states' peoples' representatives were not included among the states' members of the Constituent Assembly. It was against the declared principle of the All India States' Peoples' Conference and the Congress which had been insisting that all the representatives of the states to the Constituent Assembly should be elected by the people of the states and none of them should be the nominee of

64. *The Times of India*, 4 April 1947.

65. *White Paper on Indian States*, p. 31.

66. Ibid.

the princes.[67] The dubious[68] role played by the Congress was criticised by Jaya Prakash Narayan, Secretary of the Congress Socialist Party.[69] He exhorted the All India States' Peoples' Conference to demand full and unfettered representation of the people.[70]

On 17 April addressing the All India States' Peoples' Conference at Gwalior, Nehru admitted that the compromise formula was not wholly satisfactory. He clarified that the Constituent Assembly being a creation of the Cabinet Mission Plan was bound by its limitations. The question, therefore, was "not what was desirable or desired but what was possible and practicable under the circumstances."[71] Nehru also declared that any state which did not come into the Constituent Assembly would be treated by the country as a hostile state and such a state would have to bear the consequences of being so treated.

The Muslim League took strong exception to Nehru's speech, and send a prompt rejoinder from Liaqat Ali Khan, one of the member of its Central Executive, who in a press statement declared that the Congress had no right to coerce the states and that the states were perfectly within their rights in refusing to have anything to do with the Constituent Assembly. He appealed to the states to "disregard the idle threat."[72] Moreover, Jinnah, its supreme leader, emphasised that the states were to be independent with the termination of British paramountcy.

---

67. *Leader*, 6 March 1947.
68. Vanaja Rangaswami, *The Story of the Integration*, op. cit. p. 197.
69. Ibid. Later J.P. became a Sarvodaya leader and a leading light in independent India.
70. *Leader*, 6 March 1947.
71. Ibid. 20 April 1947.
72. V.P. Menon, op. cit. p. 78.

The attitude of the Muslim League encouraged many princes to think of independence and of forming a "Third Force" and emboldened them not to join the Constituent Assembly. But at the same time it led many others to feel the need of a strong central government after the end of the British rule.[73] Consequently a large section of the Indian princes joined the Constituent Assembly against the wishes of Bhopal.

73. Urmila Phadnavis, *op. cit. p. 173.*

7

The Indian States on the Eve of Independence

Another important development was taking place at this juncture. The rulers and their advisers had for some time been thinking of regional federations of the states. The Jam Saheb of Nawanagar and the Maharaja of Dhrangadhra took considerable interest in the formation of a union of the Kathiawar states. Some of the rulers of central India had appointed a special committee to from a draft constitution for their region. In regard to the Punjab states two draft schems prepared respectively by the rulers of Bahawalpur and Mandi were discussed. The Raja of Baghat had drawn up a scheme for a Punjab Hill States union. The rulers as well as the ministers of some of the states in Rajasthan had proposed a scheme for the union of all the Rajput states. Some of the rulers of the Deccan states had agreed to form a single union. The rulers of the Orissa and Chattisgarh states were discussing the idea of an Eastern States Union.[1]

The chamber of the princes was toying 'with the idea of setting up of a confederation of states. It might be, they

1. V.P. Menon, op. cit. p. 78.

thought, the alternative for safeguarding the rights and privileges of the states irrespective of their area, size, population and revenue.[2]

The confederation scheme was vehemently criticised by the Congress as well as by the States' people. Gandhi personally was averse to the suggestion, for he had a suspicion that the proposal had been instigated by the Political Department. Nehru was not opposed to the idea of their grouping themselves into a union, but he, first, wanted each ruler to grant responsible government to his people. Later, in a speech at the All India States' Peoples' Conference, Nehru said that the states which could not possibly form economic units should be absorbed into the neighbouring provinces and not with other states.[3]

The confederation did not fulfil certain basic principles for such a grouping and therefore was "hollow and impracticable"[4] First, the territories of confederating states were interspersed with those of British India, and important states did not join it. Secondly, the proposed confederation also lacked linguistic unity. Thirdly, it "was vested" with those powers which the confederating states did not exercise till now, e.g., currency, coinage and broadcasting.[5]

The scheme was therefore only an attempt on their part to keep jointly the autocratic power which they found could no more be kept individually.[6] There were anti-confederation agitations in Rajputana, Nawanagar and Kathiawar.

Except for the short-lived unions of the Deccan states,

---

2. Urmila Phadnavis, op. cit. p. 174.
3. V.P. Menon, op. cit. p. 79.
4. K. Santhanam, "A Reactionary Plan", *Hindustan Times*, Delhi, 13 April 1947.
5. *Free Press Journal*, 5 April 1947.
6. Ibid.

the Simla Hill states and the eastern states, none of these schems ever came into being.[7]

Meanwhile the Political Department was busy devising measures for its own liquidation. As a first step, a conference of Residents and political officers was held in the second week of April 1947 to consider steps for the contraction of paramountcy and its eventual lapse. The Secretary of State had given the viceroy maximum discretion in carrying out the policy of relaxation of paramountcy with a view to the greatest possible devolution by the end of 1947, subject to the avoidance of any step which might prejudice the future unity of India in regard to defence and communications. The object, as explained by the Political Adviser to the Conference, was to enable the states to stand on their own feet, to encouroge them to hold together and at the same time to co-operate fully with British India. The programme was to withdraw Political Agents by the Autumn and the Residents by the end of 1947, while the main duties of the Political Department were to be wound up by the end of March 1948.[8]

It was about this time that Lord Mountbatten, the last English viceroy, announced the plan of 3 June 1947, according to which the dominions of India and Pakistan would be established long before June 1948 and that the question of Indian states would be dealt with in the light of the Cabinet Mission's memorandum of 12 May 1946.[9] The very next day in a press conference it was also declared by Mountbatten that the British Government would relinquish power by 15 August 1947, and the British Paramountcy would lapse on that date.[10]

---

7. V.P. Menon, op. cit. p. 79.
8. Ibid.
9. Mountbatten, *Time only to Look Forward: Speeches 1947-48*, Nicholas Kaye, London, 1949, pp. 13-18.
10. V.P. Menon, op. cit. p. 84.

These announcements stirred both British India and the Indian states. Some of the rulers continued to favour independence after the transfer of power without bothering about the geographical and economic compulsions and implications of such a move. Bhopal, Hyderabad. Travancore etc., were some of those states who thought in such terms.[11] Many still hopes to form a Third State—a 'Statistan'. The Jam Saheb of Nawanagar was one of its protagonists. A great majority of the states became increasingly conscious of the need of accession to the new dominions.

Even amongst those who were convinced that geographical conditions required them to join either India or Pakistan, there were considerable differences. While the politically conscious amongst them, such as Bikaner and Patiala, stood for accession to the Indian union with a strong centre at Delhi, others like Jodhpur and Junagadh seemed prepared to be lured to Pakistan by Jinnah. According to V.P. Menon's version, the ruler of Jodhpur was given a blank paper duly signed by Jinnah in which he asked the ruler to fill in any concessions he wanted.[12] Where geographical situation permitted option to join either of the two dominions, religious sentiments and the will of the people played no insignificant role in determining the rulers' attitude. The Hindu and the Sikh subjects of the Indian states wished to built up a strong centre. The Muslims of the Indian states were divided in their opinion. They were unhappy over the possibility of any conflict between India and Pakistan, but while on the one hand some nationalist Muslims believed in joining hands with India, others like the Ittehad-ul-Muslimeen of Hyderabad dreamt of independence.

The Maharaja of Patiala ultimately refused Jinnah's offer[13] and the Maharaja Kumar of Jaisalmer was led to say

---

11. K.M. Munshi, *The End of An Era*, pp. 38-39.
12. V.P. Menon, op. cit. pp. 116-17.
13. His Highness the Maharaja of Patiala, 'I remember....', *The Tribune*, Ambala, 19 July 1959.

to Jinnah that his state might join Pakistan in case the latter promised that if there was any Muslim uprising in his state against the Hindus, he would side with the Hindus. When there was a conflict between his religious feelings and the people's will, the Nawab of Junagarh decided in favour of the former and joined Pakistan; but the Maharaja of Jodhpur, who had seemed receptive to allurements of Jinnah to join Pakistan, ultimately consented to join the Indian dominion under the pressure of the will of the people, including the *jagirdars* and the *thakurs* of his state who refused to link themselves to a Muslim state.[14]

The differences among the rulers of the states almost wrecked the chamber of princes and made it impossible for them to function collectively in those momentous days. Soon after the announcement of the plan, the Nawab of Bhopal resigned his chancellorship of the chamber of princes. In a letter to the viceroy, he stated that "the state of Bhopal does not wish to remain associated in any manner whatsoever with the Chamber of Princes or any of its subordinate organisations" and that it would "negotiate direc twith the successor governments of British India in regard to its interests and its future political relationship with Pakistan and Hindustan."[15]

On the resignation of the Nawab of Bhopal as chancellor, the Maharaja of Patiala, then Pro-chancellor, took over the chancellorship. As a matter of fact, the whole organisation was in chaos. It was later decided by the Standing Committee that the chamber would be wound up as soon as paramountcy lapsed.[16] There was, however, a section of the rulers who still felt that a strong and effective organisation in the place of the chamber was necessary.

For this purpose, the states entitled to separate representation in the Constituent Assembly, known as 'viable

14. V.P. Menon, op. cit. pp. 116-7.
15. Ibid. p. 84.
16. III (b) 83 of 1947, Patiala Archives, Chamber Section.

states' with the exception of a few states like Bhopal, Travancore and Hyderabad began discussions to form an organisation succeeding the chamber. However, the smaller states became apprehensive regarding the attitude of the major sta es. This suspicion and conflict of interests stood in the way of the establishment of an organization to succeed the chamber of princes, and with the crystallization of group alignments, the chances of any concerted action on the part of the rulers as a body receded. Though the constitution was drawn up, nothing concrete emerged beyond that.[17]

The June Declaration had its own impact on the All India States' Peoples' Conference and Praja Mandals associated with it. Their reactions to the situation were almost similar to those of the Indian National Congress. Like the latter, the former accepted partition as a bitter pill and felt convinced that the partition demanded all the more a strong centre at Delhi, the immediate accession of the states to the Indian dominion and its reorganisation into viable federal units. The All India States' Peoples' Conference consented to merge its identity with the Congress and the latter recognised the Praja Mandals associated with the All India States' Peoples' Conference as its branches. The integration of these popular bodies of the states with the Congress strengthened the bond of unity and enabled the Congress leaders to promote the accession of the states to the Indian dominion.[18]

Thus the partition plan strengthened the idea that there should be a strong centre at Delhi and generated a strong feeling in a large section of the rulers and peoples of the states in favour of integration.[19]

With the announcement of the partition plan several problems—legal, constitutional and political—cropped up.

17. V.P. Menon, op. cit. p. 85.
18. Urmila Phadnavis, op. cit. pp. 181-82.
19. Ibid. p. 182.

The fundamental among these for the states was the fate of paramountcy after the transfer of power. A great deal of controversy raged around it. Obviously, the British did not wish it to be transferred to the successor government. All the same, it was high time to decide whether paramountcy should lapse on the transfer of power to the successor governments or it should lapse earlier. But by far the most important question was whether, even after the relinquishment of paramountcy by the British, the Indian government could claim certain paramountcy over the states by virtue of its actual political position in the country and, if this was not possible, how were they to be tied in a bend necessary for peace and harmony.[20]

The very concept of the lapse of paramountcy was, however, repugnant to the Congress. It became more so after the rulers of Bhopal,[21] Hyderabad,[22] and Travancore[23] declared that, after the lapse of paramountcy, their states would be independent and sovereign. Jawaharlal Nehru, provoked by the statements like these, declared in a meeting of the All India Congress Committee on 15 June that, though paramountcy as vested in the crown might lapse or "return to the states" there was a "certain inherent paramountcy in the Government of India which cannot lapse...because of the very reasons of geography, history, defence, etc."[24] He warned those states who were unwilling to join the Indian union that they could not live "in void"[25] and they must come to some arrangement with the union. The relationship would be "not one of equality but slightly lower." Nehru categorically stated that these "arrangements cannot possibly admit of the right of a state to any contact with any foreign state", as "we

---

20. Ibid.
21. Menon, op. cit. p. 80.
22. Ibid. p. 84.
23. *The Nation*, 6 June 1947; and *The Times of India*, 13 June 1947.
24. S.L. Poplai, *India*, 1947-50, vol. I, Oxford University Press, Bombay, 1959, p. 168.
25. Ibid.

cannot permit anything to happen in India in any state which affects fundamentally the security of India, either in relation to defence arrangements or in relation to contact with foreign powers."[26] Finally, he maintained that the independence of any such state was not to be recognised by India, and the recognition of such independence by any foreign power would be considered an "unfriendly act."[27]

The All India Congress Committee, in the same session, passed a lengthy resolution repudiating the claim of any state to declare independence and to live in isolation from the rest of India. It also maintained that the relationship between the Government of India and the states would not be "exhausted by the lapse of paramountcy." The lapse "does not lead to the independence of the states."[28]

The All India States' Peoples' Conference, which by this time had almost identified itself with the Congress, affirmed its stand in the matter.[29] In Hyderabad the State Congress challenged the Nizam's declarations in favour of independence.[30] The Travancore State Congress demanded referendum on the issue and threatened to launch a *satyagraha* if the ruler of the state did not choose to accede to the Indian union.[31]

Jinnah, on the other hand, contested the Congress thesis. In a statement issued on 18 June, he unequivocally declared that, constitutionally and legally the states would be independent sovereign states on the termination of paramountcy and that they would be free to adopt any course they liked. He thought that the Cabinet Mission's memorandum did not in any way limit their choice to the extent that they had no

---

26. Ibid.
27. *The Hindu*, Madras, 17 June 1947.
28. *The Times of India*, 13 June 1947.
29. Ibid, 27 June 1947.
30. *The Leader*, 29 June 1947.
31. V P Menon, op. cit. p. 91.

option except to join one or the other Constituent Assembly.[32] He considered them free to remain independent if they so desired. Neither the British government, nor the British Parliament, nor any other power or body could compel the states to do anything contrary to their free will and accord, nor had they any power or sanction of any kind to do so.[33] Further, in his correspondence with Sir C.P. Ramaswami Aiyer, he agreed to have diplomatic relations with Travancore after the transfer of power.[34]

The British government's attitude on the question of paramountcy was identical with that of Jinnah. Mountbatten, however, made it clear that, after the transfer of power, though the states were free "to enter either Constituent Assembly or make such other arrangements"[35] as they deemed necessary, they could not "enter the Commonwealth separately as Dominions."[36] This stand of the British government, which was reiterated consistently till the transfer of power, limited considerably the freedom of choice before the states and discouraged to a great extent a certain section of the rulers including the Nawab of Bhopal, the Jam Saheb of Nawanagar and the ruler of Indore who intended to execute independent treaties with the dominion governments and desired the recognition of their independent status by Britain as well as the U.S.A.[37]

The constitutional aspect of the lapse of paramountcy came into focus in the course of the drafting of the Indian Independence Bill. The British government wished to

---

32. *The Leader*, 27 June 1947.
33. V.P. Menon, op. cit p. 91.
34. Mountbatten, op. cit. p. 39.
35. Ibid.
36. Parliamentary Debates, House of Commons, vol. 439, 1946-47, 23 June-11 July 1947, His Majesty's Stationery Office, London, 1947, col. 2452; *The Hindu* 16 July 1947.
37. Menon, op. cit. p. 101.

terminate paramountcy and agreements through a provision in the Indian Independence Bill. V.P. Menon, the Constitutional Adviser to the Indian government, on the contrary thought that since "the exercise of paramountcy was not based on any legislation by parliament, its withdrawal need not be by means of parliamentary legislation." He also felt that there were several important agreements which had been entered into "for the common benefit of the states and British India where paramountcy did not enter," and that "the mutual rights and obligations of the parties under agreements could not be regarded as lapsing on the withdrawal of paramountcy."[38]

The Secretary of State decided to stand by his opinion and suggested that the sub-clause (b) of the section 7 of the Bill should be as follows :

> "(b)...the suzerainty of His Majesty over the Indian states lapses, and with it, all treaties and agreements in force at the date of the passing of this Act between His Majesty and the Rulers of Indian states, all functions exercisable by His Majesty at that date towards Indian states or the Rulers thereof, and all powers, rights, authority or jurisdiction exercisable by His Majesty at that date in or in relation to Indian states by treaty, grant, usage, sufferance or otherwise."[39]

Mountbatten showed the draft Bill to the leaders of the Congress and the Muslim League in order to elicit their views. The Muslim League had no comments to offer on the aforesaid provision. The Congress leaders wanted a specific provision in the Bill for the accession of the states which was conspicuous by its absence. They strongly protested against the comple abrogation of the treaties and agreements with the states on the ground that it would result in "administrative

38. Ibid.
39. *Indian Independence Bill* (Indian Reprint), Government of India Press, Delhi, 1947, Clause 7 (b).

chaos of the gravest kind."[40] They maintained that negotiations with a "large number of states would necessarily be a long and laborious task" and wished it to be provided in the Bill that, "untill new arrangements are completed, the existing relations and arrangements between His Majesty's Government and any Indian Ruler in all matters of common concern shall continue as between the two Dominion Governments and the state concerned."[41]

Mountbatten felt that "the unconditional lapse of treaties and agreements would hit the states equally hard" and recommended that the aforesaid proviso be added with some "time limit, say 31 March 1948" for its operation.[42]

The Secretary of State was opposed to the inclusion of the proposed provision in the bill on the grounds that it would be hardly legal for the British parliament to place obligations on the Indian states without their consent, and hardly proper for the British government to fix different dates for relinquishing power in British India and terminating paramountcy over the states.[43] Ultimately he agreed to insert the following proviso at the end of that clause :

> "Provided that, notwithstanding anything in paragraph (b) or paragraph (c) of this sub-section, effect shall, as nearly as may be continued to be given to the provisions of any such agreement as is therein referred to which relate to customs, transit and communications, posts and telegraphs or other like matters, untill the provisions in question are denounced by the Ruler of the Indian state or person having authority in the tribal areas on the one hand, or by the Dominion or Province or other parts

40. Menon, op. cit. p. 104.

41. Ibid. pp. 104-5.

42. Ibid. p. 104.

43. Ibid.

thereof concerned on the other hand, or are superseded by subsequent agreement."[44]

The Congress leaders also regretted that there was no specific provision in the Bill for the accession of the states and wished a specific provision for the purpose in clause 2 of the Bill. The Secretary of State consented to insert at the end of clause 2 that "without prejudice to the generalisation of the provisions of sub-section (3) of this section, nothing in this section shall be construed as preventing the accession of Indian States to either of the New Dominion."[45]

The Political Department[46]

The Congress leaders were not happy with the attitude of the Political Department which was more interested in devising measures for its own liquidation than in solving the problems which were to arise out of the lapse of paramountcy. As a first step, a conference of Residents and Political officers was held in the second week of April 1947 to consider the steps for the contraction of paramountcy and its eventual lapse which included the withdrawal of Political Agents and Residents from the states, the handing over of cantonment areas and the crown Representative's Forces to the various states, and the ultimate winding up of the main duties of the political department. The department had also begun to destroy its records. All this alarmed the Congress leaders. On 11 June the Standing Committee of the All India States' Peoples' Conference demanded that either the political department and its agencies should be handed over to the new Government of India or a new Central Department should be created immediately to discharge the functions of the political department.

---

44. *Indian Independence Act*, op. cit. clause 7.
45. Ibid. clause 2.
46. The material under the heading is largely drawn from V.P. Menon, *The Story of the Integration of Indian States*, pp. 79-95.

The question was raised by Jawaharlal Nehru in a meeting of party leaders held on 13 June 1947.

Nehru agreed with Mountbatten that the political department would automatically close down with the lapse of paramountcy but he pointed out that all the other functions of the political department with the exception of paramountcy would be required to be dealt with by the Government of India. This led to a discussion on the precise nature of extra-paramountcy functions of the department as well as the formations of a machinery for dealing with the matters of common concern between the states and the successor governments.

Mountbatten in this context brought forward two alternatives suggesting that the states should be given option of (a) dealing with local representatives of the successor governments, or (b) appointing representatives of the states at the headquarters of the successor governments. These alternatives, Mountbatten felt, should be put before the states. He had discussed in London the question of the Government of India taking over the residencies in the various states. His instructions had been that this was only to be done if the states agreed.

Mountbatten was supported by Conrad who held that as the states were not likely to agree to have the Agents of the Government of India, "each state or a group of states should appoint a representative, or representatives, to be located at the headquarters of the appropriate government."

Nehru thought that these suggestions proceeded from a wrong basis. He insisted that the present arrangements should continue as before. He also said that any opposition "to the policy of the Central Government, that would be considered as an unfriendly act and all the privileges which such a state enjoyed would cease."

Mountbatten said that he recognized the rights of the two new governments to set up a new department of their own to deal with the states' matters, but this should not be called 'the Political Department'. A more acceptable name would be 'the states Department.' It was to be divided into two sections, one of which was to be headed by a Congress leader and the other by a Muslim League leader.

Powers and Functions of the States Department : As no states' representative was invited to this meeting, it created considerable apprehension and dissatisfaction in the minds of the rulers. The chancellor sent telegrams to the viceroy, expressing their fears. In reply, the viceroy sent the chancellor a copy of the proceedings of this meeting and Nehru in a separate letter assured the Maharaja that the formation of such a department was only "an attempt to avoid the void that would be created by the ending of the Political Department."[47] It was only a machinery to be used by the Government of India to transact its own business with greater efficiency.[48] It had nothing to do with the final settlements and states' interests were not to be affected by it at all.[49] In this conference, it was also agreed that while ephemeral records and documents might be destroyed by the Residents, the crown Representative's records might be weeded and sorted out with the assistance of the experts appointed for the purpose by the Member for Education in the Interim Government.

The State Department came into being on 27 June 1947, with Sardar Patel and Abdul Rab Nishtar as heads of its two sections and V.P. Menon as its Secretary.

Patel issued a statement on 5 July appealing to the rulers to join the Indian union on three subjects—defence, foreign affairs and communications. He pointed out that "it

---

47. Jawaharlal Nehru's letter to Patiala Maharaja, VII (a) 31 of 1947 (extracts), Patiala Archives Chamber Section.
48. Ibid.
49. Ibid.

is an accident that some live in the states and some in British India, but all alike partake of its culture and character. We are all knit together by bounds of blood and feeling no less than of self-interest. None can segregate us into segments : no impassable barriers can be set up between us...I hope the Indian States will bear in mind that the alternative to co-operation in the general interest is anarchy and chaos which will overwhelm great and small in a common ruin if we are unable to act together in the minimum of common tasks."[50] Referring to the lapse of paramountcy he hoped that it would not be the desire of the rulers to utilise "this freedom from domination" in such a manner as would be injurious to the common interests of India.[51]

The States Department was mainly confronted with two problems. First, it had to weld the 652 states with the Indian dominion and, secondly, to find a method of implementing the various agreements between the Indian states and the British government after the paramountcy had lapsed. It was also to find some sort of a substitute to fil up the vacuum that would be created by the dissolution of Residencies and withdrawal of Political Agents and Political officers.[52]

As regards the question of the future relationship of the states with the successor government, it was thought that some sort of an Instrument of Accession, based more or less on the model of the draft Instrument of Accession of 1935, might be prepared.[53]

So far as the princes were concerned, the question of the mode of establishing their relationship with a free India was discussed by them as early as 1946 in its Constitutional Affairs

---

50. Menon, op. cit. p. 100.
51. V. Patil, *On Indian Problems*, Publications Division, Delhi, 1949, p. 3.
52. Urmila Phadnavis, op. cit. p. 191.
53. Ibid.

Secretariat. The Special Drafting Committee of the Chamber of Princes, in its meeting of July 1946, said that the individual states or the groups of states, should join the Indian union through some formal treaties.[54] But, in January 1947, the Private Secretary to the Maharaja of Patiala, in a note, stated : "It is doubtful if it will be constitutionally appropriate for the states to accede to the union by executing treaties with the union. Treaties are agreement between different states. The union constitution will not represent a treaty between the states and British India but it will be a constitution drawn up jointly by the British Indian Provinces and Indian states... As compared with treaties, Instrument of Accession offers a more suitable alternative."[55]

The difference of opinion among the princes conformed to a pattern : the Bikener—Patiala Group, willing to join the Constituent Assembly, favoured an Instrument of Accession whereas the Nawab of Bhopal, who was unwilling to accede, preferred treaty agreement.[56]

In order to work out various commercial, economic and financial agreements Mountbatten suggested some sort of Standstill Agreement. But no final decision could be arrived at and it was agreed that the matter should be referred to a meeting of the representatives of states and of British India to be held sometimes in July.[57]

On 10 July a number of rulers and states' ministers met at the Sardar's residence. It was attended by Rulers of Patiala and Gwalior, Sir B.L. Mitter of Baroda, K.M. Pannikar of Bikaner and Hari Sharma of Patiala. The Sardar urged that the states which had joined the Constituent Assembly should forthwith accede to India on three subjects,

---

54. VII (a) 14 of 1947, Patiala Archives, Chamber Section.
55. Ibid.
56. Urmila Phadnavis, op. cit. p. 191.
57. Menon, op. cit. pp. 85-90.

and pointed out that such a course would enable them to have a direct voice in shaping the policies of the Central Government. The states' delegation while favouring the Sardar's plea emphasised that the matter required careful consideration and cautions approach and necesssitated informal discussions between the rulers and their advisers on the point.[58]

The next day the State Department issued the agenda for the conference of the rulers to be held on 25 July 1947 : (1) The accession of the states on defence, external affairs and communications (2) The Stand-still Agreement; (3) The Advisory Council for the States Department; (4) The Channels of correspondence and the representation of the Central Government in the states.[59]

On 24 July the Sardar and V.P. Menon met another delegation of rulers and the states' ministers which included the Rulers of Patiala, Gwalior, Bikaner and Nawanagar, Sir A. Ramaswami Mudaliar (Mysore) and Sir C.S. Venkatachari (Jodhpur). Apparently quite a number of rulers had broken away from the leadership of the Nawab of Bhopal and were prepared to come into the Indian union.[60] By this time the States Department had already produced a draft Instrument of Accession and revised the original draft of the Standstill agreement prepared by the Political Department. These two drafts had already been circulated among the princes at an informal meeting of the chamber on 25 July in which Mountbatten addressed that chamber for the first and last time in his capacity as Crown Representative.

Mountbatten advised the rulers to accede to the appropriate dominion in regard to the three subjects : (a) defence, (b) external affairs, and (c) communications. He said that accession on these three subjects left the rulers with all the

58. Ibid. p. 107.
59. Menon, op. cit. p. 107.
60. Ibid p. 108.

practical independence that they could possibly use and made them free of those subjects which they could not possibly manage on their own. He assured them that their accession on these subjects would involve no financial liability and that in other matters there would be no encroachment on their sovereignty. Finally, he appealed to them to join either of the two dominions before 15 August 1947.[61]

In order to expedite the work, the Negotiating Committee was split into two sub-committees to deal respectively with the Standstill Agreements and the Instruments of Accession.[62] A joint meeting of these sub-committees was held in the Bikaner House on 31 July 1947, which prepared the draft of Instrument of Accession and Standstill Agreement which were eventually approved by the General Conference of the Chamber of Princes on 1 August 1947.[63]

Instruments of Accession

The Instruments of Accession were not uniform for all the states. In the case of 140 rulers, who were the members of the Chamber of Princes, the Instruments of Accession provided accession to the Dominion of India on the three subjects of defence, external affairs and communications.[64] In the case of the estates and *talukas* of Gujarat which were attached to the adjoining bigger states but which desired their position to be reverted after the lapse of paramountcy, another Instrument of Accession was drafted which vested all the residuary powers and jurisdiction in the Central Government.[65] Subsequently an ordinance termed as the "Extra-Provisional Jurisdiction ordinance" was promulgated for the exercise of powers and jurisdiction acquired by the Government of India in these areas.[66] In the case of a number of intermediary states

61. PA. CH. VII (a) 38 of 1947.
62. PA. CH. VII (a) 32 of 1947.
63. Ibid.
64. *White Paper on Indian States*, pp. 156-8 and 165-8.
65. Ibid.
66. Menon, op. cit. p. 110.

which were higher in status than the estates and *talukas* of Kathiawar and enjoyed wide but not quite full powers, still another Instrument of Accession was signed with the object of ensuring that they did not enjoy more powers than they had before 15 August 1947.[67]

Standstill Agreement

The Standstill Agreement, however, was identical in all cases. It laid down that all agreements and administrative arrangements as to the matters of common concern specified in the schedule then existing between the crown and the states should continue "untill new arrangements in this behalf" were made.[68] The Agreement excluded the exercise of any paramountcy functions by the Central Government.[69] The States Department further assured the Chancellor that "all the personal privileges of the rulers as at present existing, whether covered by the Standstill Agreement or not, would be respected by the Dominion Government."[70]

With this began a series of meetings in which the Viceroy persuaded the rulers to join either union as early as possible. Some of the rulers were inclined to execute Standstill Agreements and then wait and see, as far as the Instrument of Accession was concerned. It was, however, made clear to such rulers in a conference on 1 August 1947, that the Government of India had decided to execute Standstill Agreements with only those who had already signed the Instrument of Accession.[71]

The States Department then began negotiations with all the states for their accession. While it was easy to deal with

---

67. Ibid.
68. *White Paper on Inc ian States*, pp. 173-4.
69. Ibid.
70. PA. CH. VII (a) 21 of 1947.
71. PA. CH. VII (a) 32 of 1947.

the states which were concerned of the inevitability of accession, it was most difficult to tackle those who had declared that they would be independent after the transfer of power or for some reason or other favoured the accession to Pakistan. When the States Department invited Travancore to attend the conference of rulers on 25 July 1947, its Dewan, Sir C.P. Ramaswami Aiyer, promptly replied that there was no point in his attending the meeting as it had decided not to accede to India. He, however, responded to Mountbatten's invitation and came to Delhi. In his discussions with V.P. Menon on 20 July[72] and with Mountbatten on 21 July[73] all the important points advantageous to the Travancore state were explained to him. Ultimately, he promised to take the Maharaja the draft of Accession and a letter from Mountbatten. Soon after his return to Travancore, an assault was made on his person and in the meantime the Maharaja of Travancore telegraphically informed the Indian Government of his acceptance of both the Instrument of Accession and the Standstill Agreement.[74] As pointed out earlier, Jodhpur could also be ultimately persuaded to execute the Standstill Agreement and the Instrument of Accession with the Indian dominion.

Bhopal-Indore group did attempt to negotiate with some foreign powers with a view to getting international recognition to their states as independent and sovereign states but, after the accession of Travancore along with many states and in view of the strong public reaction to their declaration, they realised that they could not survive for long outside these dominions. Bhopal ultimately acceded to India. Gradually, even the "last ditchers" like Dholpur, Indore, Bharatpur, Bilaspur and Nabha signed the Instrument of Accession with the Indian union.[75]

---

72. *Hindustan Times*, 22 July 1947.
73. Menon, op. cit. p. 116.
74. Ibid. p. 120.
75. Ibid.

Some rulers signed the Instrument of Accession and forwarded it with covering letters which laid down the conditions subject to which the accession had been signed. The Government of India insisted that the accession of the states could be accepted only unconditionally, and ultimately they complied with this.[76]

Thus, before 15 August 1947, all the states except Junagarh, two small states under the Muslim rulers of Kathiawar, Kashmir and Hyderabad, acceded either to India or Pakistan. In view of the peculiar problems and special position of Hyderabad and Kashmir, the offer of accession was kept open to them even after 15 August 1947. Kashmir announced its willingness to negotiate a Standstill Agreement with both India and Pakistan on 12 August 1947 and three days later an agreement with Pakistan was signed. The Maharaja's offer the sign a Standstill Agreement stood with India for some time and it was neither accepted nor rejected by the Government of India.[77] In the case of Hyderabad, however, no agreement was reached with the Government of India and on 12 August 1947, Mountbatten informed the Nizam that the offer of accession would remain open for Hyderabad for a further period of two months.[78]

However, after the raid of the tribals Pakistan on Kashmir, the Maharaja, with the concurrence of the President of the National Conference, Sheikh Abdullah, signed the Instrument of Accession with India on 26 October 1947.

In Hyderabad, the public opinion was divided : While the majority favoured unity with the Indian union, a strong minority under the leadership of Kasim Rizvi continued to

---

76. Ibid.
77. *White Paper on Jammu and Kashmir*, Government of India Press, Delhi, 1948, pp. 2-3.
78. *White Paper on Hyderabad*, Government of India Press, Delhi, 1948, pp. 1-40.

dream of an independent Muslim state of Hyderabad and was aggressively hostile to the Indian union. The hostile designs of such a powerful minority had to be overcome by the police action before the Nizam consented to accede to the Indian union.

Thus, as Mountbatten aptly said in the Constituent Assembly on 15 August 1947, with the accession of the states, a "unified political structure" was established in India. The stage was now set for the final phases of integration.

Conclusion

Though the points of contact between British India and the princely states were many, the latter were slow in assimilating the new principles and ideas, methods and practices current in the former. But the growing influence of the modern conditions of life gradually broke down the isolation of the states from one another and from the rest of India. New forces of constitutional development and national movement posed problems which could not be solved by keeping India divided into two water-tight compartments.

From Lytton in the 1870s to Hardinge in the second decade of the 20th century repeated attempts were made to organise the Indian princes as a conservating bloc against the Indian nationalist movement. The British government countered the nationalist movement by playing two trump cards : one was that of the Muslims, and the other that of the states. The princely order was unduly sensitive about its privileges and prerogatives, and laid claim to the status of sovereignty, often verging on the exercise of a despotic rule over their subjects. Their pretensions came directly into conflict with the principle of democracy, solicitude for the rights of the people and sentiments of the unity of India so fondly cherished by nationalist India.

The relationship between the princely states and British India during the period 1919-47 was influenced to a large extent by the pressure exerted by these various factors; and the constitutional proposals which evolved were often a compromise between conflicting aims of the British government, the princely order and the nationalist movement. These constitutional proposals laid increasing stress on the union of both the Indias as the solution of India's manifold problems. The concept of a union or united states of India like Alwar, Bikaner and Baroda, a 'sisterhood of states', a 'federation' and a 'council of greater India' as propounded in the reports of official and non-official committees and commissions, consistently maintained the need for constitutional inter-relationship between the states and the rest of India. The conflict of interests, however, on the part of the parties concerned—the Princes, the Paramount Power and the Political Parties in India—made its realisation well-nigh impossible.

The British government used the states as a conservative group dependent on paramount power and bound to follow the imperial policy, thus neutralising the Congress. When in the 1930s the British under the pressure of Indian Liberals agreed to the idea of an Indian federation they saw to it that if at all the federation came into existence, it would be controlled by them and not by the Congress. The princes in the initial stages believed that their entry into the federation might, among other things, mean a release from the clutches of the Political Department, but they soon realised that what the Congress had envisaged as a federation was likely to result in a question of the right of the States' System.

The period under review also witnessed the states' peoples' movement on a large scale. There had been demonstrations, uprisings and agrarian troubles in some of the states even earlier. But such moves, though directed against the administration of the state in question, were not motivated by the ideal of freedom or the desire on the part of the people to take over the reigns of the administration in their own hands. Coming to this period one finds a change in the mood of the states' people. Having realised that they could improve their lot only by replacing the autocratic rule in the states by some kind of popular administrations. In harbouring this aspiration and in launching their campaign the states' people found the example of the Indian National Congress handy.

Indeed, the movement in the states ran along two parallel lines at the same time: The first related to the demand for a responsible government and the second was an extension of the British Indian anti-imperialistic struggle. But this distinction was purposely submerged by a leadership within the states which sought to gain a wider base to its cause, and more particularly all India sympathies in its favour. The all-India leadership, on the other hand, entered the states' sphere mainly to counteract the British machinations which sought to prop up the princes against the nationalist forces. Thus, this leadership, though it sought to use the forces so unleashed in the states in their ambitions on a democratic programme towards their own programmes of union and integration, did seek to hold itself aloof from an active involvement in the states' peoples' movement for a responsible government.

The Congress had full sympathy with the states' people in their struggle, but they were not prepared to interfere with the internal affairs of the states. For the first time, the Congress at its Calcutta session of 1928 assured the princes of its sympathy and support in their struggle for the attainment of their legitimate aims. Closer understanding between the Congress and the states' peoples' movement was further widend in the countrywide non-cooperation campaigns launched by the Congress under the supreme leadership of Gandhi. The pressure from within the form of the states' peoples' movement compelled the unwilling and recalcitrant princes for accession to the Indian union on the eve of Indian independence.

The British had a curious love-hate relationship with the princes. They tried to play both the crescent card and the states' card. If the British had tried to fulfil their obligations to everybody in India, they would have lived longer than they did. The more they played the crescent card, the more difficult it became for them to play the states' card effectively.

They fulfilled their obligations to the Muslims to a large extent, but they had to ditch the princes.

The interactions of various forces after the second world war, like the socio-political movements within the states; the attitude of the state governments towards them; the attitude of the Indian National Congress towards them; the relations between the States' Peoples' Movement and the Indian National Congress and the policy of the paramount power towards the Indian states, helped the process of the integration of the states with the Indian union.

Indeed, Sardar Patel, by his firm and tactful handling of the problem succeeded in integrating the Indian states to the Indian union, thus reviving the traditional unity of our country. Mountbatten also helped in some ways: When Bikaner was vacillating in 1947, he steadied him. He even goaded the Prime Minister of a prince to sign the Instrument of Accession.

The patriotism and self-sacrifice of many of the Indian princes was commendable. For example, the Rulers of Jodhpur, Bikaner and Jaisalmer. Indeed, the young Ruler of Jaisalmer refused to be duped and befooled by Jinnah. Similarly, when in June-July 1947 the Nawab of Bhopal was playing his tricks and creating confusion all around, it was the enlightened leadership provided by Baroda, Bikaner and Patiala which tilted the balance in favour of the states joining the Dominion of India by signing the Instrument of Accession. There has been no dearth of emigres working against their own countries, but no Indian ruler really turned traitor to his country.

APPENDICES

APPENDIX I

REPRESENTATION OF 'LESSER STATES' IN THE CHAMBER OF PRINCES*

Statement showing the Recommendations made by the Committee of Princes for the Grant of Representation in the Chamber of Princes to "Lesser States"

Names of States	*Area in Sq. miles*	*Population*	*Approximate annual revenue (Rs.)*	*No. of Representatives*	*Remarks*
1	*2*	*3*	*4*	*5*	*6*
Bombay					
I. Kathiawar States : Seventeen 3rd and 4th Class States :					

* Progs. C. of P. 1921-28, 9-10.

(Contd.)

	1	2	3	4	5	6
	Lakhtar, Sayla, Chuda, Vala, Jasdan, Manavadar, Thana-Devli Vadia, Lathi, Muli, Bajana, Virpur, Malia, Kotda-Sagani, Jetpur, Bikha, Patdi	1,949	198,865	1,947,000		
II.	Northern States :					
	Pol, Kadana, Tharad	1,525	73,950	171.895		
III.	Central States :					
	Bhor, Akalkot, Anundh, Phalton, Jath, Surgana	3,662	452,483	1,804,194		
IV.	Southern States:					
	Miraj (Senior), Miraj (Junior), Jamkhandi, Kurundwad (Senior), Namdurg, Savanur	1,483	310,041	1,791,754		

Madras				
Sandur	167	13,526	81,614	
Punjab				
I. Plain States : Padaudi, Kalsia, Dujana	320	100,010	510,509	
II. Simla Hill States : Baghai, Baghat, Balsan, Bashahr, Bhajji, Bija, Darkuti, Dhami, Jubbal, Keonthal, Kothar, Kumharsain, Kunihar, Mailong, Mangal, Nalagarh, Sangri, Taroch	5,153	300,000	1,200,000	2
Bihar and Orissa				
Orissa States :				
Patna, Kalahandi, Sonpur, Bamra, Rairakhol	9,871	1,300,000	1,440,000	1

(*Contd.*)

1	2	3	4	5	6
Gangpur, Bonai, Mayurbhanj, Keonjhar, Dhenkanal, Baud, Khandpara, Daspalla, Nayagarh, Talcher, Nilgiri, Hindol, Athmallik, Ranpur, Narsingpur, Athgarh, Pal Lahara, Barmoa, Tigiria					
Chotanagpur States:					
Seraikela and Kharsawn	18,777	2,640,000	5,390,000	2	
Central Provinces					
Bastar, Kanker, Surguja, Udaipur, Jashpur, Raigarh, Sarangarh, Makrai Sakti, Kawardha Khairagharh, Korea, Nandgaon, Chhuikhadan, Changbhakar	31,081	2,109,121	3,640,583	2	

Central India				
(a) Gwalior States :				
Khaniadhana				
(b) Bundelkhand States :				
Sarila, Beri, Bihat, Gerauli,				
Gaurihar, Banka-Pahri,				
Bijna, Dhurwari, Tori,				
Fatehpur, Jigni, Lugasi, Alipura, Nai-gawan rebai				
(c) Beghalkhand States :				
Nagod, Baraundha, Jaso, Kothi, Sohawal, Bhaisundha,				
Pahra, Paldeo, Tarson, Kamta, Rajaula				
(d) Bhopal States :				
Kurwai and Mahammadgarh				
(e) Malwa States :				
Piploda, Panth Piploda				
(f) Southern States :				
Jobat, Kathiawara, Mathwar, Ratanmal, Jammia, Nimkhera	2,483	331,374	1,247,000	1

APPENDIX II

CHAMBER OF PRINCES

Members of the Standing Committee—A Chart*

Salute	*21*	*19*	*17*	*15*	*13*	*11*	*9*	*Total*
February 1921	Gwalior	—	Cutch Patiala Bikaner*	—	Nawa-nagar	Jhalawar Palanpur	—	7
November 1921	Gwalior	—	Bikaner* Cutch Patiala	Alwar	Nawa-nagar	Palanpur	—	7
February 1923	Gwalior	—	Patiala Bikaner* Cutch	Dholpur	Nawa-nagar	—	—	7
November 1924	Gwalior	—	Patiala Bikaner*	Alwar Dholpur	Nawa-nagar	—	Sangli	7

January 1926	—	Kashmir	Bikaner Patiala*	Alwar Dholpur	Nawa-nagar	—	Sangli	7
November 1926	—	Bhopal Kashmir	Patiala* Cutch Bikaner	Alwar	Nawa-nagar	—	—	7
February 1928	—	Bhopal Kashmir	Patiala* Bikaner Cutch	Alwar	Nawa-nagar	—	—	7 plus 6 Substitute Members-Dholpur, Jodhpur, Kapur-thala, Palanpur, Panna and Sangli.
February 1929	—	Kashmir** Bhopal	Patiala* Bikaner Cutch	—	Nawa-nagar	—	Sangli	(7 plus 6) 13 Substitute

(*Contd.*)

Salute	*21*	*19*	*17*	*15*	*13*	*11*	*9*	*Total*
								Members-Dholpur, Jodhpur, Porbandar, Rewa, Sawant-wadi, and Sitamau
February 1930	—	Kashmir** Bhopal	Patiala* Bikaner	Alwar Dholpur	Nawa-nagar	—	—	13 (7 plus 6) Substitute Members-Sangli, Jodhpur, Rewa, Panna,

								Sitamau, Wankaner
March 1931	—	Bhopal*	Patiala** Cutch** Bikaner	Alwar Dholpur	Nawa-nagar	—	—	12 (7 plus 5) Substitute Members-Porbandar, Sangli, Dungarpur, Maler-kotla and Rewa
March 1932	—	Bhopal	Cutch** Bikaner Patiala	Dholpur Alwar Dungar-pur	Nawa-nagar Jhalawar	Panna	Sangli	11

(Contd.)

Salute	*21*	*19*	*17*	*15*	*13*	*11*	*9*	*Total*
March 1933	—	—	Bikaner Bahawalpur Patiala	Alwar Dholpur** Dungarpur	Jhalawar Rampur	Panna	Wankaner Sangli	11
January 1935	—	—	Bikaner Bahawalpur Patiala*	Dewas (jr.) Dungarpur Dholpur	Jhalawar	Panna Mandi	Sangli Wankaner	11 (including Chancellor and Pro-Chancellor)
February 1937	—	—	Bahawalpur	Dungarpur	Nawanagar**	Bilaspur Mandi	Wankaner Sachin	11

	Bikaner Jodhpur Patiala*	Sangli
March 1939-46 :	Since March 1939, as the Standing Committee of the recognised Chamber was on a regional basis, there were no elections.	

* Progs. C. of P. 1921-37.

* Chancellor

** Pro-Chancellor

APPENDIX III

COMMISSION OF ENQUIRY AND THE STATES*

Cases in which the British Government offered the Appointment of a Commission of Enquiry to the Rulers

Indore : Early in 1926 the Maharaja Tukeji Rao of Indore was offered a Commission of Enquiry to investigate the question of his connection with the conspiracy by certain officials of the State to kidnap Mumtaz Begum, His Highness' favourite dancing girl, culminating in the murder of Sheikh Abdul Qadir Bawla in Bombay. His Highness, however, declined the offer and proposed to abdicate provided the enquiry was abandoned. This was accepted by the Government of India.

Bharatpur : Recently the Government of India, as the result of the indebtedness of the State due to the extravagance of the Maharaja and general maladministration in the State, offered a Commission of Enquiry to the Maharaja. The offer was refused by His Highness, who left the administration entirely in the hands of His Excellency the Viceroy. His Highness has been advised to entertain an European Dewan selected by the Government of India and to delegate to him full powers of administration, and to abstain from issuing orders direct, except in the case of minor departments.

Nabha ; In 1922 there were serious allegations of oppression and methodological perpetration of injustice by the Maharaja of Nabha under the cover of legal forms. A Special Commissioner was appointed to enquiry into these allegations, and, as a result of his report, His Highness the Maharaja of Nabha was permitted to sever his connections with the State

---

*Indian States Committee, *Oral Evidence recorded before the Committee* (for official use) 104-6 (extracts).

on certain terms. The following are the more important of these conditions :

(1) The administration of the State will be handed to the Government of India, and the Maharaja will formally abdicate in favour of his son when the latter comes of age;
(2) The Maharaja will in future reside outside the State on an allowance from the State;
(3) That the Nabha State will pay a substantial sum to the Patiala Durbar by way of compensation;
(4) His Highness' visit to certain specified places will require the previous permission of the Government of India; and
(5) That the Maharaja will remain subject to the obligation of loyalty and obedience to the British Crown and the Government of India.

These conditions were subject to annulment or modification in event of failure to fulfil any obligation

APPENDIX IV

POSITION OF INDIAN STATES

Legal Opinion of the Joint Counsel on the Position of Indian States vis-a-vis British Government, and the Comments of the Indian States' Committee centre as well as the Nehru Committee on it.

LEGAL OPINION ON THE COUNSEL

The main conclusions of the memorandum submitted by the joint counsel to the Indian States Committee were as follows :

(1) The relationship between the Crown and the various States (which were originally independent) was 'legal, importing definite rights and obligations on both sides.'

(2) The Indian States possessed all original sovereign powers, except in so far as any had been transferred to the Crown. Thus, 'the complete sovereignty of the State is divided between the State and the Crown' with the States having residuary jurisdiction.

(3) This transfer had been effected by the consent of the State concerned, and in no other way.

(4) The consent of a State to transfer sovereign rights of the Crown was individual to that State, and the actual agreement made by the State must be investigated to see what rights and obligations had been created.

(5) Such agreement appeared normally in a treaty or other formal engagement. An agreement to transfer sovereign powers was, however, capable of being made informally. In such cases the onus was on the transfer, viz., the Crown, to prove the agreement.

(6) The relationship of the Crown as Paramount Power and the State was one involving mutual rights and obligations. In this context Paramountcy was not a factor creating rights or obligations but 'merely a name for a certain set of rights when vested by consent in another sovereign State.' Consequently Paramountcy gave to the Crown definite rights and imposed upon it definite duties in respect of certain matters like foreign affairs, internal and external security etc. It, therefore, did not confer upon the Crown any authority or discretion to do acts which were not necessary for the exercise of such rights and the performance of such duties.

(7) The mutual rights and obligations created by treaty and agreement were between the State and the

> British Crown, i.e., the King in his British or, it may be, in his Imperial Capacity, and not with the King in the right of any one of his dominions.

Finally, "the British Crown has this in common with a corporation that by its nature it must act through individuals; but where it has undertaken obligations, and duties which have been entrusted to it by the other contraction party in reliance on its special characteristic and reputation, it must carry out those obligations and duties by persons under its control; and cannot delegate performance to independent persons nor assign to others the burden of its obligations or the benefits of its rights. So the British Crown cannot require the Indian States to transfer the loyalty, which they have undertaken to show to the British Crown, to any third party, nor can it, without their consent, hand over to persons, who are in law or fact independent of the control of the British Crown. the conduct of the States' foreign relations, nor the maintenance of their external or internal security."

While agreeing with the joint counsel that the relationship of the States was with the British Crown and not with the Government of India, the Butler Committee refuted their basic assumptions regarding the sovereignty of the States. It maintained that, historically, the States were not independent and sovereign when they came into contact with the British Power. 'In fact, none of the States ever held international status. Nearly all of them were subordinate or tributary to the Moghul empire, Maratha supremacy or the Sikh Kingdom, and dependent on them.' Further, while agreeing with the counsel that the treaties between the Paramount Power and the States should not be read as a whole, the Butler Committee refused to accept the argument of the Joint Opinion that only agreements between the States and British Government were the source for determining their relationship. According to the Committee, this relationship was not a mere contractual relationship, resting on treaties made more than a century ago but was the product of change and growth, depending on treaties, engagements and *sanads* supplemented by usage, sufferance and political practice. Thus the theory of limited Paramountcy agreement as enunciated at the joint counsel was unsupported by evidence. Nor was the contention of the counsel regarding Paramountcy giving to the Crown definite rights and obligations in regard to certain matters only was correct unless these matters, according to the Committee, "are made to cover all those acts which the Crown…his considered necessary for imperial purposes, for the good government of India as a whole, the good government of individual States, the suppression or barbarous practices, the saving of human life end for dealing with cases in which rulers have proved unfit for their position."

This all-pervasive nature of Paramountcy prompted the Butler Committee to conclude that Paramountcy was indefinable as it had to adapt itself in accordance with the circumstances and situations developing in the States and outside.

While elucidating the limitations on the sovereign powers of the Princes, the Indian States Committee reminded the Princes that the Princes should not resent the Paramountcy of the Paramout Power, for, if it provided checks on their powers it also protected them against 'the danger of destruction' from within as well as without. It was in this context that the Paramount Power was prepared to retain them under its protective umbrella by agreeing to their demand that the relationship of the States with the Paramount Power could not be substituted by the relationship with a new government in British India responsible to an Indian legislature without their consent.

NEHRU COMMITTEE REPORT

The conclusion of the Butler Committee as well as of the joint counsel of Indian States having direct relationship with the Crown and not with the Government of India was challenged by the British India. Commenting on this, the Nehru Committee report maintained that this proposition was "untenable historically and legall." In actual practice it was the Government of India and not the Crown with which the

Rulers came into direct contact and the Political Secretary of the Government of India practically discharged all the functions pertaining to Indian States as there was no separate member in charge of political portfolio. Further, in the theory of "personal relationship and personal confidence and the consequent duty of paramount power remaining in India to discharge its obligations,"the British India statesmen envisaged an attempt on the part of Paramonntcy to keep the two Indias separate from each other and to nullify their demand of 'dominion status' for the whole of India. They therefore requested the Princes not to be led by legal ingenuities but by broader considerations of national interests. They also warned the Rulers that such theories were "fraught with mischievous possibilities which could only lead to disaster" in future.

APPENDIX V

CONFEDERATION SCHEME*

Memorandum by His Highness the Maharaja of Indore, His Highness the Maharaja Rana of Dholpur, Nawab Liaqat Hayat Khan and Sir Prabhashankar Pattani.

The Future constitution of India has been the subject of close examination by many able and eminent authorities, and as it was considered necessary to bring about a union between British India and the Indian States for determining the policies in regard to subjects of common concern, and execution and administration thereof, various methods for bringing about that unity have been explored, and proposals formulated

*Indian Round Table Conference (Second Session), *Proceedings of Federal Structure Committee and Minorities Committee* (London, His Majesty's Stationery Office, 1932) 518-9.

during the past few years. At the Round Table Conference held last year, however, the suggestion to bring about such a union on the Federal basis took more definite shape and the deliberation of the Conference proceeded on the basis that the future constitution of India should be of a Federal type embracing both British India and the Indian States. The precise form and structure of the new Federal Government, as rightly stated inter alia by the Prime Minister in the declaration made by him on behalf of His Majesty's Government on January 19th, 1931, was to be determined after further discussion with the Princes and representatives of British India.

The Conference has resumed its work and the Federal Structure Committee is now engaged in formulating the precise form and structure of the new constitution in all the minute details. This must naturally require working out and evolving a scheme that might be acceptable to the various interests concerned.

To secure the support and adherence to it, the constitution must take due note of all the various standpoints on the several details and provide for them adequately; failing that, it would not have the necessary support, and, consequently, would not work successfully, and if it is pushed through under pressure, it is likely to do more harm than good.

The Federal Structure Committee outlined, after their deliberations last year, a scheme for the proposed future Federal Constitution for India. Details on important points were left over for further consideration last year and they are being taken up now. As I was not then a member of the Round Table Conference, and had no occasion to communicate my views to the Indian States' Delegetion or the Conference, I consider it advisable for me to express my views at this stage on the several important points at issue, and take this opportunity of placing them on record for consideration.

In introducing the scheme hereafter stated, I shall add one observation viz., that the future constitution for all India on the Federal basis will have to be on the basis suited to the peculiar conditions in the country, and not on the basis of the constitution of a Federal type existing in other countries. If no two of those constitutions are exactly alike, there is greater reason and justification for India with her peculiar conditions and a large variety of interests (e.g., non-autonomous Provinces and Sovereign Indian States) to evolve our own scheme and a constitution which would be suited to, and satisfy the requirements of, the several interests, and varying and peculiar conditions and sentiments of the people and their Princes.

In my opinion, the main features of the constitution should proceed on the following lines :

(1) Federated British Indian Provinces, i.e., British India and the States collectively.

The States will, with the assent of the Crown, constitute themselves into an Electoral College which may be given any suitable name, i.e., all the States will make one group or unit for the purpose of electing their quota of representatives to the Federal Legislature.

(2) Federation to be for purposes of specified matters of common interest only.

(3) Functions, Policy and Legislation in regard to, and administration of, certain specified subjects, as detailed in Annexure A.

Note : The Federal Legislature will lay down policy and enact laws relating to the subjects enumerated in Annexure A.

The States will, then, automatically pass the Federal Laws as State Laws and they will then come into force within the territories of the States.

In the event of failure on the part of any State to carry out the policy and laws passed, the Confederation of States will use its influence and bring round the defaulting State through its representatives; but even if that fails, which is not likely, the Federal Government will take necessary action through the Crown.

(4) Structure and Composition of the Federal Government : (a) Legislature. There should be preferably only one Chamber, to which representative could be sent by States through the Electoral College referred to above. The representation of the Indian States should be 50 per cent. If it is bicameral, the States should have 50 per cent representation in the Upper Chamber and on population basis in the Lower Chamber.

(b) Execution. (1) The States need not insist on a fixed number of representatives in the Federal Executive. (2) The Executive will be responsible to the Legislature.

(5) Method of Election of States Representatives. The States will constitute themselves into a Confederation for the purpose of Federation with British India. This will serve as an Electoral College for electing their representatives to the Federal Legislature. The Confederation will be composed of representatives of Sovereign States and of groups of the remaining States.

Major states may be allotted a fixed number of seats to ensure their individual representation, and some regional distribution may also take place. For the purposes of election the principle of plural voting may be accepted, the number of votes allotted to particular state depending on the State's political position, though population and income may also be given due weight. The details will be settled by the States themselves.

The representatives constituting the quota of the States will represent the States collectively and they will include among them representatives of major states for whom seats will be reserved.

(6) Federal Finance. Federal finance will be found from indirect taxation only, so far as at least the States are concerned.

(7) Supreme Court and Arbitration Court. There should be a court to deal with constitutional questions only. In case the volume of work does not justify the constitution of a permanent court, provision should be made for the constitution of a Court each time as the occasion arises but the qualifications of the eligible personnel and the method of its constitution shall have to be specifically and definitely laid down in the constitution.

For disputes between the Crown and the Indian States, provision should be made that they shall be settled by an Impartial Court of Arbitration distinctly separate from the Federal Court, the constitution of which should also be defined beforehand. The Arbitration Court should also decide disputes between a State or States and Provinces inter se, or between a State or States and Central Government of British India. Neither the Federal Court nor the Court of Arbitration shall exercise jurisdiction as the highest Court of Appeal.

ANNEXURE-A

No. in Devolution Rules	*Subject*
1	2
5. (a) Railways	Federal, for Policy and Legislation. Administration to be Federal only for through lines
(b) Aircraft and all matters connected therewith	Do

(*Contd.*)

1	2
(c) Inland waterways, etc.	Federal, for Policy and Legislation in respect of inland waterways affecting more than one component State.
6. Shipping and Navigation etc.	Federal, for Policy and Legislation.
7. Lighthouses, etc.	Federal for Polioy and Legislation.
8. Port Quarantine and Marine Hospitals	Federal as far as internation requirements are concerned.
9. Ports	No special opinion.
10. Posts, telegraphs, telephones, including wireless installations	Posts, telegraphs, trunk telephones and wireless installaions to be Federal but with such quantifications as may be necessary for the purpose of adjustment with the States in matters of detail.
11. Custom	1. Maritime Customs : Federal, subject to special rights and obligations under treaties, agreements and engagements with the Maritime States. 2. On external fronteirs of India : Federal, subject to special case of Kashmir.
Salt	Federal, subject to the existing rights of the Indian States.
12. Currency and Coinage	Federal, subject to adjustment, with the states concerned, of such rights as are not already conceded by them.

(*Contd.*)

1	2
14. Saving Bank	Post Office Savings Bank : Federal for Policy and Legislation.
15. Indian Audit Dept.	Federal, Audit to be Federal.
21. Control of Cultivation and Manufacture of opium, Sale of opium for export.	Federal for Policy and Legislation.
22. Stores and Stationery required for Imperial Departments	For Federal Departments to be Federal.
24. Geological Survey of India	Federal.
26. Botanical Survey of India	Federal.
27. Inventions and Designs	Federal for Policy and Legislation.
28. Copyright	Federal for Policy and Legislation.
29. Emigration from and Immigration into British India	Emigration from and immigration into India : Federal for Policy and Legislation.
31. Central Police Organisation	Federal, Police to be Federal
35. Survey of India	Federal.
38. Meteorology	Federal.

(*Contd.*)

1	2
39. Census Statistics	Federal for Policy and Legislation.
40. All India Service	Federal, Services should be Federal.
44. Immovable Property, etc.	Immovable property acquired and maintained at the cost of Federal Government should be Federal.
45. Public Service Commission	Federal for the purpose of Federal Services.

Note : The remaining subjects should not be federalised.

APPENDIX VI

PRINCES AND THE FEDERATION*

Resolution passed by a Meeting of Indian Princes and Representatives held at Bombay on the 25th February, 1935

The Princes and the representatives of the States present at this meeting have examined the Government of India Bill and the draft Instrument of Accession and read and considered the Report made by the Committee of Ministers presided over by Sir A. Hyderi which has recently dealt with some of the

*Views of Indian States : Correspondence relating to a Meeting of States' Rulers held at Bombay to discuss the Government of India Bill and a Provisional Draft Instrument of Accession (Delhi, Government of India Press, 1933) 11.

important provisions of the said Bill and draft Instrument of Accession. They have also considered the opinions of legal advisers and experts whose views have been obtained thereon. While reserving to themselves the right to offer further observations and criticisms in due course, the Princes and the representatives of the States present at this meeting fully endorse the observations and criticisms contained in the Report submitted by the Committee of Ministers to the extent that the Committee have been able to deal with the matters in question.

This meeting desires to emphasise that in many respects the Bill and the Instrument of Accession depart from the agree ment arrived at during the meeting of representative of the States with members of His Majesty's Government, and regrets to note that the Bill and the Instrument of Accession do not secure those vital interests and fundamental requisites of the States on which they have throughout laid great emphasis.

This meeting is of the definite opinion that in their present form, and without satisfactory modification and alteration on fundamental points, the Bill and Instrument of Accession cannot be regarded as acceptable to Indian States.

APPENDIX VII

Lord Irwin's Note on the General Principles of Administration in the States*

1. The function of the government may be described as the task, firstly, of ensuring to the individuals comprising the society the opportunity of developing hemselves as human beings, and secondly, of moulding them into a compact and contented state. The discharge of this double function involve the necessity of finding and maintaining the due balance between the rights of the individual and those of the State to which he belongs.

2. The life of a community depends upon being regulated not by the arbitrary will of individuals but by Law, which should expressly or tacitly be based upon and represent the general will of the community.

This is equally true of Autocracy, Oligarchy, and Democracy.

And the efforts of Rulers therefore, whether they be one or many should be directed to the establishment of Reign of Law.

3. The application of these principle supplies among other needs :

(a) Protection of individual life, liberty, and property, etc.

(b) The provision of adequate machinery for the adjustment of dispute among individuals.

(c) The provision of adequate machinery of justice i.e., proper code of law, law court, appeals, etc.

(d) The recognition of the equality of all members of the State before the law.

4. These things depend upon :

(1) An administration conducted in accordance with law.

(2) An efficient and uncorrupt police force.

(3) An efficient judicial system, strong in personnel, who are secure from arbitrary interference by the executive and are secure in the tenure of their office so long as they do their duty.

5. The fundamental principle of State in I implies that government must follow definite principles in :

(a) the collection of revenue from its subjects

(b) the expenditure of revenue so collected.

6. Revenue : Taxation should be :

(a) as light aspossible.
(b) easy of collection.
(c) certain i.e. the tax-payer should be able to forecast his liability.

(d) proportionate to the means of tax-payers to pay.

7. Expenditure : From this it follows that the proportion of revenues allotted to the personal expenditure of one ruler should be as moderate as will suffice to maintain his position and dignity, in order that as large a proportion as possible may be available for the development of the life of community and its individual citizens. The civil list of an enlightened modern ruler is formally fixed at either a definite sum or a definite percentage of the total income of the state.

8. Under the General head of development fall :

Education.

Health.

Agriculture.

Housing etc.

The devolution of many such subjects and local bodies make for good government.

9. Government must be, by the nature of its task, responsible and not irresponsible in character.

In democracy, it is responsible to a wide electorate.

10. Every government should have some machinery by which it can inform itself of the needs and desires of its subjects and by which these can make their voice heard.

These machinery need not be strictly representative (or elective) in character, but its essential requisite is that it should maintain a close connection between government and governed.

11. There are other matters, such as religious toleration, the encouragement of mutual confidence and harmony

between the employee and employed, in which government may not be able to make effective use of law, but in which it is nonetheless bound to direct its influence towards the preservation of friendly and neighbourly relation between the different component parts of the single unit of the state.

12. Perhaps the principal necessity for a ruler is that he should be able to choose wise counsellors and, having chosen them, he should trust them.

APPENDIX VIII

CO-OPERATIVE GROUPING*

The attitudes of the Princes on the question of co-operative grouping has been authoritatively stated in our reply to His Excellency's opening address during the last Chamber session. We recognise the desirability of taking suitable action, where needed, to ensure efficiency of administration and we feel that this can be done on a voluntary basis without impinging on the sovereignty of the States concerned. As such we should like to elucidate certain points which appear to require further consideration.

(a) What is the criterion of the basis under which States are invited to co-operate for certain administrative purposes ?

(b) With regard to the proposed scheme of joint police force, the following points need clarification—

(1) That the extent to which the police force would discharge the function of the Paramount Power in

---

*FPF No. 34(3), Political Secret, 1940, 16.

protecting that State concerned, that part of expenditure should be borne by the Paramount Power as has been done in Neemuch.

(2) Is there any objection to associate a committee of Rulers or ministers with the presidents to advise the Resident with regard to the functioning and control of the joint police force ?

(c) What would be the inter-relation of the local and joint police force when both are operating in the same sphere of action ? Who will control them ?

(d) What is the object of the proposed Intelligence Scheme and how is it intended to work ?

(e) What is the objection to the proposal that the State so desiring may arrange either with their adjoining important States or with retired judges to high court or retired senior district or session judges to come to the State for a certain number of days during the month or in the quarter, to dispose of those appeals, which would ordinarily go to a high court in British India ?

The Princes feel that, since the objective in view can be achieved through cordial advice and on a voluntary basis, this should be encouraged in preference to imposing any scheme without regard to the special condition of the State concerned.

APPENDIX IX

ATTACHMENT OF STATES ACT*

An Act to Render Legal the Attachment of Certain Indian States to Other Indian States

1. *Attachment of States* : (1) At the instance or with the consent of His Majesty's Representative for the exercise of the functions of the Crown in its relations with Indian States, any Indian State not mentioned in Divisions I to XVI of the Table of Seats appended to Part II of the First Schedule to the Government of India Act, 1935 (25 Geo. V & I Edw. VIII, c.2) (as in force at the passing of this Act), being a State included in the Western India States Agency or the Gujarat States Agency on the 25th day of August 1943 may be attached to any other Indian State and, in connection with the attachment, provision may be made for :

(a) the exercise by, or transfer to, courts and officers of the last-mentioned Indian State, with or without limitations or conditions, of any powers or jurisdiction in or in relation to the first-mentioned Indian State which were or could have been exercised by or on behalf of the Crown therein before the attachment ;

(b) the relinquishment, as a consequence of the attachment, of any such powers or jurisdiction of the Crown as aforesaid ;

(c) the transfer of cases pending at the date of the attachment before courts or officers of the Crown ; and this subsection shall have effect notwithstanding anything in the Foreign Jurisdiction Act, 1890 (53 & 54 Vict., c. 37), the Government of

*Gwyer, M., and Appadorai, A., ed., *Speeches and Documents on Indian Constitution* 1921-47, Vol. II (London, Oxford University Press, 1957) 762-3.

India Act, 1935 (26 Geo. V. & I Edw. VIII, c. 2), any other Act for the time being in force, or any Letters Patent, Order in Council or other instrument.

(2) This section shall be deemed always to have had effect : Provided that His Majesty's Representative for the exercise of the functions if the Crown in its relations with Indian States may give such directions, if any, as he thinks proper for rendering valid or lawful anything done or omitted before the passing of this Act which would otherwise be invalid or unlawful by virtue of the provisions of this section.

2. *Short title.* This Act may be cited as the India (Attachment of States) Act, 1944.

APPENDIX X

FUTURE GOVERNMENT OF GREATER INDIA: QUESTIONS POSED BY THE RULERS*

General

We are prepared to discuss and negotiate the future Government of Greater India. You can count upon our whole-hearted co-operation and goodwill and if necessary, even sacrifice as we consider necessary for the immediate attainment by India of her full stature.

Constitution Making Body

1. What will be the composition of the proposed constitution-making body and what will be its functions ? The question of procedure will, of course, have to be settled later.

---

*P.A CH. VII (a) 16 of 1957.

2. Is it to discuss the future Government of British India or its component units ? If so, we cannot be expected to participate in it just as we would not like British Indian interference in our internal arrangements.

3. Whatever the form and functions of the proposed body, we take it as understood:

(a) that it will not be free to discuss questions relating to the continuance of monarchical from of Government of ruling dynasty in each State :

(b) that its decision affecting the States will be subject to ratification by them.

4. We are glad to endorse the statement of Secretary of State in regard to representation of the State subjects in these discussions. The question of association of non-official elements in the States with the co-operation of the States on the court-making body is a question for the decision of the Rulers and State Governments concerned.

INTERIM ARRANGMENTS

1. Whether interim arrangements contemplated are for the Government of British India alone or for the whole of India ?

2. Would the functions of Governor-General and the Crown Representative continue to be separate and will they be discharged by two separate persons on one person ?

3. What would be the position regarding Paramountcy during the interim period ?

4. Separate machinery will have to be devised for :

(a) matters exclusively concerning States in the sphere of Paramountcy ;

(b) matters of common concern with British India.

5. Is it proposed to pursue the interim arrangements even if there is no settlement in regard to bigger issues?

6. Will the British Government in the interim period be responsible to the legislature or to Governor-General?

GENERAL QUESTION

1. Is India to be absolutely independent or will she have some connection with the Crown?
2. What will be the position of States in an independent India? Would they be free to negotiate separate treaties with (a) Government of Britain, (b) British India?
3. If there is complete independence, will Britain be prepared to defend India? If so, on what terms?
4. In the proposed treaty between Government of Britain and the future India Governmen tor Governments, do you propose making any provision in regard to treaty obligation to the States?
5. In case British India decide on more than one India, we presume that the discretion of the States will be unfettered to join one or the other or to stand aloof or to have a confederation of States which may so desire.

Note II

I

(a) The States will not hamper nor stand in the way of complete self-government or independence being granted by the British Government to India.

(b) In a free India, whatever the form of government, there will be no room for Paramountcy. The relations between the new Indian Government and the States will be regulated on the basis of mutual agreement or treaties.

(c) In any treaties that are made or sought to be made between both the present British Government and the new Government of India, the Indian States should be fully and adequately consulted.

II

(a) The monarchical form of government and the continuance of the ruling dynasty in each State should not be affected by the new scheme.

(b) The Indian States will exercise full rights of internal administration but will be willing to arrive at an agreement with British India for the purpose of a Central authority charged with the formulation of policies and with the administration of subjects of common interest like defence, external affairs, communications, sea customs, tariffs. The Central authority should preferably be a body representing the new government in British India and the government of States, the representation to be in such manners as may be decided upon by mutual consultation and agreement.

III

The states, as such, do not propose to take part in question relating to the internal administration of the provinces in British India or in the discussions relating to Pakistan, Sikhistan, Dravidstan etc. Persons appearing before the Cabinet Delegation, of course, are entitled to express their personal view without committing the States as such.

IV

With regard to internal administration of the States, there will be no dictation or interference either by the British Government or by the new government except that steps should be taken for the attainment of a definite standard of association of the people with the government, to be arranged for by the States themselves with due advertence to local circumstances. A removable executive on the model of British Parliament should not be regarded as either essential or necessarily suited to the conditions of India.

Bibliography

ORIGINAL SOURCES

A. Government Records—National Archives of India

Foreign and Political Departmental Records
Home Political Records
Fortnightly Reports
Crown Representative Records, available in microfilm.

B. Printed Matter—Government Publications and Records

C.L. Tupper (compiled), *Indian Political Practice—A Collection of the decisions of the Government of India in Political Cases*, 1895, vols. 1-4.

W.W. Hunter (ed.) *Imperial Gazetteer*, vol. XVIII, published by Government of India.

Memoranda on the Indian States—1926, 1930, 1932, 1934, 1936, 1937 and 1940.

Report on Indian Constitutional Reforms (1918).

Montagu Chelmsford Reforms—Chapter X, Government of India publications, 1918.

Papers relating to the Sixth Despatch on Indian Constitutional Reforms (1919) Chapter X in 1919 Act.

Report of the Indian States Committee (1928-29), Published by Government of India.

Report and Evidence of the Indian States Committee (1927), (1927-29), 4 volumes.

W.W. Nind, *Report of the Special Committee on Economic and Financial Relations between British India and Indian States.*

J.C. Davidson, *Constitutional Reforms—Indian State Enquiry Committee*, 1931.

Views of Indian States; Correspondence relating to a meeting of States' Rulers held at Bombay to discuss Government of India Bill and Draft Instrument of Accession, 1935.

Round Table Conference proceedings, India Office Stationary :

(a) *Indian Round Table Conference Proceedings*, 12 November 1930 to 19 January 1931.

(b) *Indian Round Table Conference Proceedings of Sub-Committee I (On Federal Structure)*, 12 November 1930 to 19 January 1931.

(c) *Indian Round Table Conference Report—Refer Reports of Committee on Federal Structure*, Reports, I, II and IV.

(d) *Indian Round Table Conference, Second Session Proceedings of the Plenary Session*, 7 September 1931 to 1 December 1931.

(e) *Indian Round Table Conference, Second Session, Proceedings of Federal Structure Committee*, 7 September 1931 to 1 December 1931.

(f) *Indian Round Table Conference—Second Session, Federal Finance Sub-Committee—Stenographic notes on the meeting of the Sub-Committee* at St. James Palace on 28 September 1931 (No mention of this meeting in other proceedings).

Joint Committee of the Indian Constitutional Reforms—Report 1933-34—Proposals for Indian Constitutional Reforms, White Paper, 1933.

Secretary of States Evidence Before the Joint Committee on Indian Constitutional Reforms, 2 volumes (1933)

Debates on Indian Affairs, House of Commons Session, 1935.

Parliamentary Debates Official Report (1936).

Government of India Act 1935.

Report of the Committee Appointed to Negotiate with the States Negotiating Committee (1946-47).

Indian Independence Act (1947)

V. T. Krishnamachari, *Ministry of States on Indian States Finance Enquiry Interim and Final Reports in two parts*, 1948.

White Paper on the States published by the Ministry of State, Government of India (1950).

N. V. Gadgil : *Enquiry on Special Assistance to Part B States Ministry of States*, 1953.

All India Credit Survey—Survey Report of the Committee of Directives, vols. I, II and III (1954).

Parliamentary Debates, House of Commons for relevent periods.

C. Unofficial Papers

Organisation :

All India Congress Committee Paper, NMML (1857-1947)
All India States' Peoples' Conference Papers, NMML (1934-1947).

D. Private Papers

Indian Leaders and Administrators

R. R. Diwakar Papers

Tarachand Papers (History of Freedom Movement Unit)

Jawaharlal Nehru Papers.

M.R. Jayakar Papers.

Mahatma Gandhi Papers.

Mirza Ismail Papers.

Pattam Thanu Pillai Papers.

C. P. Ramaswami Aiyer Papers.

B. R. Reddy Papers.

T. B. Sapru Papers.

V. D. Savarkar Papers.

Transfer of Power, relevant volumes.

Indian National Congress Publications

Report of the All Parties Conference (Nehru Report), 1921.

Indian National Congress, Annual Reports, 1928 to 1940.

Resolutions Passed by the Indian National Congress, 1920-23, 1927, 1928, 1930-34, 1934-36 and 1941 to 1946.

AISPC Publications-General

G. R. Abhyankar, *Work in England of the Deputation of Indian States Peoples' Conference* (1929).

Memorandum presented ta the Indian States Committee by the Indian States Peoples' Conference (1928).

Address of the President, ISPC (1929).

Presidential Address to the ISPC by C. Y. Chintamani (undated).

Presidential Address to the ISPC—by R. Chatterjee, (1931).

Presidential Address to the ISPC—by N. C. Kelkar (1933).

Memorandum of the Indian States' People, presented to the Indian National Congress (1931).

Presidential Address at AISPC—by Jawaharlal Nehru (1937 and 1945).

Resolutions passed by the AISPC—1939-46.

Newspapers and Periodical –Indian and Foreign

Asia

Asiatic Affairs

Asiatic Review

Bengal Past and Present

Commonwealth

Contemporary Review

Economic and Political Weekly

Economist

Foreign Affairs

Foreign Policy Reports.
Harijan.
The Hindu.
Hindustan Times.
Historical Journal.
Indo-British Review.
Indian Annual Register (Earlier Quarterly and Half-yearly).
Indian Economic and Social History Review.
Indian Express.
Indian Journal of Political Science.
Indian Review.
International Conciliation.
Journal of Asian Studies.
Journal of Kerala Studies.
Journal of Royal Institute of International Studies.
Labour Monthly.
Liberal Magazine.
Kerala Society Papers.
Modern Asian Studies.
Modern Review.
National Herald.
New Indian Political Forum.
New India—an occasional bulletin from 1937-1939 in 2 volumes.
New India Weekly.
Political Scientists.
Rama Verma Research Institute Bulletin.
Round Table.
Servant of India.
South Asia.
South Asian Review.
Statesman.
Times of India.
United India.
Young India.

Relevent Articles Published in Periodicals

Adams, John, "Economic, Political and Social Dimensions of

an Indian State : A factor analysis for district data for Rajasthan', *Journal of Asian Studies*, November 1973.

Banerjee, Albeon 'Indian States and the Constitution Bill', *Contemporary Review*, March 1935.

Barton, William, 'The Deadlock in India and the Indian States', *Quarterly Review*, July 1943.

———, 'Princes and Politics in India', *The Asiatic Review*, October 1944.

———, 'Postwar Development Scheme in the States of South India', *Asiatic Review*, October 1945.

———, 'The Indian Princes and the Cabinet Mission', *Quarterly Review*, January 1947.

Benn, Wedgwood, Address by—at the Round Table Conference, *Journal of Royal Institute of International Affairs*, March 1931.

———, 'Accusation of Conservatives in India Again', *The Economist*, 25 November 1933.

Bhargave, Kusum, 'Rajasthan Politics and Princely Rulers'. *Indian Journal of Palitical Science*, October—December 1972.

Bikaner, Maharaja of, 'The Indian Constitution and States, *The Asiatic Review*, 12 February 1946.

Bisson, T.A., 'A New Constitution for India', *Foreign policy Reports*, 17 July 1935.

Blunt, W.S., 'Ideas About India—The Native States', *Fortnightly Review*, February 1885.

Braitsford, H.H., 'The Indian Settlement', *The New Statesman and Nation*, 25 May, 1946.

Brock, R.W., 'India, Pakistan and Indian States', *The Asiatic Review*, 1946.

Chatterjee, Ramanand, 'The Indian States', *Modern Review*, July 1931.

Chaturvedi, J.P., 'States Peoples Movement', See articles in *Mainstream* dated 14 February 1976, 28 February 1976, 6 March 1976, 3 April 1976, 8 May 1976, 19 June 1976, and 7 August 1976.

Coalman, John, 'India Today and Tommorrow', *Foreign Affairs*, 1939.

Das, Tarakanth, 'The Status of Hyderabad during and After British Rule in India', *Modern Review*, January 1949.

Darda, R.S., 'Political Movement in the Princely States of Rajasthan', *Quarterly Review of Historical Studies*, 1973-74.

Davis, Sir Godfrey, 'Kashmir a Sovereign State', *The Asiatic Review*.

Dharampal, 'British Policy Towards the Native States of India', *Journal of Indian History*, August 1947.

Dhringdhara, 'Indian Princes in the Ebb of British Retraction', *Indo-British Review*, 1973—74 (Review of Conrad Corfield's book *Princely India I Know*).

Dolobrant, Rt. Hon, Lord Llyod of, 'Problem of Constitutional Reform in India', *Journal of the Royal Institute of International Affairs*, September 1933.

Edwin, P.G., 'Travancore and Paramount Power—A Study of war time Reletionship, *Journal of Indian History*, August 1973.

Finlay, Mark, 'The Changing Role of the Indian Princes', *Contemporary Review*, October 1949.

Fisher, William, 'The Maharajas of India', *United Nations World*, 1948.

Furber Holden, 'The Unification of India, 1947-51', *Asian Affairs*, December 1951.

Gandhi, M.K., 'The Future of India', Address to the Institute on 20 October 1931, *Journal of the Royal Institute of International Affairs*, November 1931.

Garnatt, G.T., 'Indian', India *Asia*, November 1930.

Green, James Fredrick, 'India's struggle for Independence', *Foreign Policy Reports*, 1 June 1940.

Gupta, D.C., 'A Survey of the Present Constitutional Position of Indian States', *Modern Review*, September 1936.

Halifax, Viscount of, 'Indian Constitutional Reforms', *Journal of the Royal Institute of International Affairs*, March 1935.

———, 'The Political Future of India', *Foreign Affairs*, 1934.

———, 'India Two Hundred Years', *Foreign Affairs*, October 1947.

Harrison, 'Rulers and the Ruled', *South Asian Review*, October 1969.

Hydari, Sir Akbar, 'The Indian Bill Moves on', *The Economist*, 4 May 1935.

Iqbal, Ali Shah Sirdar, 'The fnture of Indian States', *The Fortnightly*, August, 1947.

James, Sir Fredrick, 'The Indian Political Scene', *International Affairs*, April 1947.

Kane, 'The Indian Problem—A Review', *Austrian Quarterly*, March 1945.

Kapadia, Rangildas, 'Rise and Growth of AISPC', *National Herald*, 24 December 1945.

Kashy, M.J., 'Political Awakening and Struggle for Freedom in Travancore', *Journal of Indian History*', August 1972.

La Foy, Margaret, 'India's role in World conflict--The Princes', *Foreign Policy Report*, 1 May 1942.

Lothian Aurther, 'A Neglected Aspect of Indian History', *Quarterly Review*, October 1962.

Nehru, Jawaharlal, 'Presidential Address—AISPC, Ludhiana, 15 February 1939, *The Settled Works of Jawaharlal Nehru*.

———, 'What of the Indian States', 27 April 1940, *J.N. Papers*, NMML.

———, 'Presidential Address, AISPC Conference, Udaipur Session, 31 December 1945, *J.N. Papers*, NMML.

Pannikar, K.M., 'The Position of Indian States—a discussion', *Asiatic Review*, 1926.

Rajagopalachari, C., 'Reconciliation in India', *Foreign Affairs*.

Reading, Lord, 'Constitutional Reforms in India', *Foreign Affairs*, July 1933.

Reed, Sir Stanley, 'The Governance of India', *Journal of Royal Institute of International Affairs*, 26 April 1927.

Retcher, William L. and Ramusack Barbara, 'The Chamber and Constitution : Changing forms of Princely Association in India', *Journal of Asian Studies*, 3 May 1975.

Rosenthal, Donald, B., 'From Reformist Princes to Cooperative Kings', *Economic and Political Weekly*, 2 June 1973.

Saklatwala Shapruji, 'The Indian Round Table Conference', *The Labour Monthly*, February 1931.

Sapru, Tej Bahadur and Khan, Zaffrullah, 'Indian Public Opinion on the White paper', *Journal of Royal Institute of International Affairs*, September 1933.

Shiva Rao, B., 'The Vicious circle in India', *Foreign Affairs*, 1941.

Singh, A. 'Twilight of the Princes', *Asia*, May 1937.

Singh, Bhupinder Singh (Maharaja of Patiala), 'The Problem of the Indian States' paper read by—*Journal of the Royal Institute of International Affairs*, November 1928.

Singh, Gurumukh Nihal, 'United States of India or Princely States', *Asia*.

Talbot, Philips, 'The Independence of India, the Indian States', *Foreign Policy Reports*, 15 June 1947.

———, 'India and Pakistan—Progress Report of Princely States', *Foreign Policy Reports*, 15 June 1949.

Venkatachar, C.S., 'Last Years of British Rule in India', *Indo-British Review*, April—September 1970.

———, 'The Unmaking of Indian Princes', *Indo British Review*, April-September 1971,

Wadia, Ramesh, 'Praja Mandal Movement in the East Punjab State', *Punjab Past and Present*, April 1972.

Walson, Sir Alfred, 'If British Quit India', *Asiatic Review*, July 1944.

———, 'India Raising up the Curtain, the Indian States', *Asiatic Review*, 1947.

Zetland, Marquis of, 'After the Indian Conference', *Foreign Affairs*, April 1932.

Unpublished Theis in Microfilm (available in NMML)

Ramusack Barbara, *Indian Princes as Imperial Politicians 1914-1939*, University of Michigan, 1969.

Books

Abhayankar, G.R., *Problem of Indian States*, Arya Bhushan Press, Poona, 1928.

Aitchison, C.U., *A Collection of Treaties, Engagements and Sanads*, Vols. IX and X, Superintendent of Government Printing, Calcutta, 1909.

———, *The Native States of India, The Principles which underlie their Relation with the British Government.*

Bagchi, Amiya Kumar, *Private Investment in India, 1900-1939*, Cambridge University Press, London, 1972.

Barton, William, *The Princes of India* (with an Introduction by Viscount Halifax), Nisbet and Company, London, 1934.

Beotra, B.R., *The Two Indias*, W. Newman and Company, Calcutta, 1927.

Bipan Chandra, *Modern India.*

Bisheshwar Prasad, *Bondate to Freedom.*

Bimal Prasad, *Gandhi, Nehru and J.P.*

Bowring, L.B., *Eatsern Experience*, King and Company, London, 1871.

Butler, Harcourt, *India Insistent*, William Heina mann, London, 1939.

Campbell, Johnson Allan, *Mission with Mountbatten*, Robert Hale Limited, London, 1951.

Chopra, K.N., *Law Relating to the protection of the Administration of States in India*, The University Book Agency, Lahore, 1940.

Chudgar, P.L., *Indian Princes under British Protection*, Williams and Norgate, 1929.

Coen, Terence Creagh. *Indian Political Service* or *Study in Indirect Rule*, Allied Publishers, Bombay, 1971.

Corfield, Conrad, *Princely India I Knew—From Reading to Mountbatten*, Indo-British Historical Society, Madras 1975.

Coupland, R., *The Cripps Mission*, Oxford University Press, London, 1942.

———, *The Indian Problem*, Part I (1933-35) and Part II (1935-42) Oxford University Press, London, 1943.

———, Future of India, Oxford University Press, London, 1943.

Das, Tarakanth, *Sovereign Rights of the Indian Princes*, Comesh and Company, Madras, 1924.

Davis Collin, C. *Memorial Volumes*—A Festschrift—with an article by Williams Donavan, 'The Adoption Despatch of 1867 and significance'. Asia Publishing House, Bombay, 1973.

Deo, N.G., *The Princes of India*, The Times Press, Bombay, Bombay, 1921.

Desai, Bhulabhai, *Speech (1934-38)*, Natesan and Company, Madras, 1938.

Dhawan, Shanti, *What are the Indian States* (Foreward by Jawaharlal Nehru), Allahabad Law Journal Press, Allahabad, 1939.

Diver, Mand, *Royal India*, Hodder and Stoughton Limited, London, 1942.

Durgadas (ed.), *Patil Correspondence, 1945-1950*, 10 volumes, Navjivan Press, Ahmedabad, 1974-75.

Edwards, Michael, *The last years in British India*, Allied Publishers, Bombay, 1963.

Fitz, Sir Kenneth, *Twilight of the Maharajas*, John Murray Limited, London, 1956.

Forbes, Rosita, *India of the Princes*, The Right Book Club, London, 1939.

Gandhi, M.K., *To the Princes and Their People*, Navjivan Press, Ahmedabad, 1940.

Gandhi, M.K., *The Indian States Problem*, Navjivan Press, Ahmedabad.

———, *Collected Works of Mahatma Gandhi*, vols. XII to XXXXIX Publication Division, Ministry of Information and Broadcasting, New Delhi.

Gauba, K.L., *His Highness or the Patholoy of the Princes*, The Times Publishing Company, Lahore, 1930.

Gundappa, D.V., *The States and Their People in the Indian Constitution*, Karnataka Publishing House, Mysore, 1931.

Gurumukh, Nihal Singh, *Indian States and British India*, Their future relations (Foreword by J.B. Sapru), Nand Kishore Bros., Banaras, 1930.

Gurjer, Maurice and Appadorai, *Speeches and Documents on the Indian Constitution (1921-47)*, 2 valumes, Oxford University Press, London. 1957.

Haksar, K.N. and Pannikkar, K.M., *Federal India*, Martin Hopkinson Limited, London, 1930.

Handa, R.L., *History of Freedom Struggle in Princely States*, (Foreward by S. Nijlingappa), Central News Agency, New Delhi, 1968.

Ismail, Mirza, *My Public Life—Recollection and Relfections*, George Allen and Unwin Limited, London, 1924.

Ismoil, Mirza, *Views and Opinions on His Retirement from Service*, Banglore Press, Banglore, 1942.

Iyengar, S. Srinivas, *Swaraj Constitution*, 1920.

Iyer, Sivaswami, *Indian Constitutional Problems.*

Jadhaw, Khaurao and Mehta, V.B., *Indian States*, Published by V.B. Mehta, Bombay, 1920.

Jarmani Das, Dewan, *Maharajas, Lives and Loves and Intrigues of Indian Princes*, Allied Publishers, New Delhi, 1969.

Kayes, J.W., *Life of Metcalfe.*

Kipling, Rudyard, *Departmental Duties and Other works.*

———, *Plain Tables from the Hills.*

Karni Singh, *The Relations of the House of Bikaner with the Central Powers*, 1865-1949, Munshi Kam Manoharlal, New Delhi, 1974.

Krishna Murthi, Y.G., *Indian States and the Feudal Plan* (with a foreward by Bhulabhai Desai), Ratausey Parker and Company, Bombay, 1939.

Kulkarni, V.B., *The Future of Indian States*, Thalker and Company, Bombay, 1944.

Lalthe, A.B., *The Problems of Indian States*, Arya Bhusan, Press, Poona, 1930.

Leewarner, William, *Native States of India*, Macmillan and Company, London, 1910.

Lord John, *The Maharajas*, Hutchinson and Company, London, 1972.

Lothian, A.C., *Kingdom of Yesterday*, John Murray, London, 1951.

Low, Sir Sydney, *The Indian States and Ruling Princes*, Earnest Benn, London, 1929.

Lumby, E.W.R., *Transfer of Power in India*, George Allen and Unwin Limited, London, 1954.

Lumby, E.W.R. and Mansergh, *Transfer of Power*, vol. I-8, His Majesty's Stationary Office, London, 1970-80.

Macmunn, George, *The Indian States and Princes*, Jarrolds, London, 1936.

Majumdar, R.C., *History of Freedom Movement in India.*

Mankekar, D.L., *Accession to Extinction*—The story of the Indian Princes, Vikas Publishing House Private Ltd., Delhi, 1974.

Mehta, Mohan Singh, *Lord Hastings and Indian States*, Taraporewala and Sons, Bombay, 1930.

Mehtab, Harekrishna, *Beginning of the End* (Foreward by Sardar Vallabhbhai Patel) Cuttack Students Store, Cuttack, 1949.

Menon, V.P., *The Story of the Integration of Indian States*, London, Orient Longmans limited, Calcutta, 1956.

———, *Transfer of Power in India*, Orient Longmans Limited, Calcutta, 1956.

Mogh, K.P., *The Indian States in their Relations with British Paramount Power and the Government of India*, K.B. Moghe, Bombay, 1928.

Montmorency, Geoffrey De, *The Indian States and Indian Federation*, University Press, Cambridge, 1942.

Moon, Penderal, *Divide and Quit*, Chatto and Windus, London, 1961.

———, *The Viceroy's Journal*, Oxford University Press, London, 1973.

Moore, R.J. (ed.), *Crisis in Indian Unity, 1917-1940*, Oxford University Press, New Delhi, 1974.

Mosley, Leonard, *The Last Days of the British Raj*, Hillman and Sons, Frome, 1962.

Narvani, D.N., *The Indian States in the Federation of India*, Karnataka Publishing House, Bombay, 1939.

Nehru, Jawaharlal, *Selected Works of Jawaharlal Nehru.* vols. 1-9 (ed. S. Gopal), Orient Longmans, Delhi, 1972-80.

———, *Unity of India*, Lindsey Drummond, London, 1941.

Nicholson, A.P., *Scraps of Paper—India's Broken Treaties, Her Princes and the Problems*, Earnest Benn Limited, London, 1930.

O'Malley, L.S.S. (ed.), *Modern India and the West—A Study of the Interaction of their Civilization*, Oxford University Press, London, 1968.

Oza Kewalram, C., *Indian States in Free India*, Vora and Company, Bombay, 1947.

Palmer, Julian, *Sovereignty and Paramountcy in India*, Stevens and Sons Limited, London, 1930.

Pandit, R.S., *Dominion Status and Indian Status*, Criticism of the Batler Committee, Allahabad, 1930.

Pannikkar, K.M., *The Evolution of British Policy Towards Indian States (1774-1868)*, Lahiri and Company, Calcutta, 1929.

———, *His Highness the Maharaja of Bikaner*, Oxford University Press, London, 1937.

———, *The History of Kerala (1498-1801)*, Annamalai University Press, Annamalai Nagar, 1960.

Pannikkar, K.M., *The Indian Princes in Council*, Oxford University Press, London, 1936.

———, *The Indian States and the Government of India*, Martin Hopkinson, London, 1932.

———, *The States and the Constitutional Settlement*, Institute of Pacific Relation International Secretariat, New York, 1942.

———, Relations of Indian States with Government of India, M. Hopkinson, London, 1927.

Pathik, Bijoy Singh, *What Are Indian States*—With illustrative documents.

Pattabhi Sitaramayya, B., *History of Indian National Congress*, vols. 1-2, Padma Publication, Bombay, 1969.

Phadnavis, Urmila, *Towards the Integration of Indian States 1919*-1947), Asia Publshing House, Delhi, 1968.

Philips, C.H. (ed.) *Partition of India*, George Allen and Unwin, London, 1970.

———, (ed.), *Selected Documents on the History of India and Pakistan*, vols. 1 to IV, Oxford University Press, London, 1970.

Puttaswami, B.S., *Should the Indian States Enter Federation*, The World Press and Publishing House, Mysore, 1935.

Raghavan, S.R.S., *The Indian States and Indian Polity* (with an introduction by G.R. Abhayankar), Indian Press, Benglore, 1931.

Raghubir Singh, *Indian States and the New Regime* (with a foreward by C.P. Ramaswami Aiyer), D.B. Taraporewala and Sons, Bombay, 1938.

Ramusack, Barbara N., *The Princes of India in the Twilight of the Empire*, Ohio State University Press, Columbus, 1978.

Ramadive, R.K., *The Legal Rights of the Indian States and of Their Subjects*—or the Truth about the Indian States, The Good Companion, Baroda, 1950.

Rangaswami, Vanaja, *The Story of the Integration—A New Integration*, Manoharlal Publications, New Delhi, 1981.

Rao, Hosakappa Krishna, *Swaraj Constitution*, Published by the Indian States Peoples Conference, Banglore, 1928.

Recluse, A., *Letters to an Indian Raja*, 1919.

Ruthuswami, M., *Relations of Indian States with Government of India*, Pearl Press, Cochin, 1931.

———, *Essays on Constitution making*, The Good Pastor Press, Madras, 1946.

Sarkar, Sumit, *Modern India*.

Sastri, K.R.R., *Indian States*, Kitabistan, Allahabad, 1941.

Sastri, V.S. Srinivasa, *The Future of Indian States*.

Sen, D.K., Indian States—*Their Status, Rights and Obligations*, Sweet and Maxwell, 1930.

Sen, S.P. (ed.), *Dictionary of National Biography*, vols. 1-4, Institute of Historical Studies, Calcutta, 1974.

Shankar, V., *My Reminiscences of Sardar Patel*, 2 volumes, Macmillan and Company, Delhi, 1974.

Sharma, Jagdish, Saran, *India's Struggle For Freedom*, 2 volums, S. Chand and Co., Delhi, 1965.

Shiva, Rao, *Framing of India's Constitution*, vols. 1-5, Indian Institute of Public Administration, New Delhi, 1966-68.

Srinivaschari, Chidambaram, S., *The Inwardness of British Annexations in India*, University Press of Madras, 1951.

Shyama Shankar, *Nature and Evolution of the Political Relations bewteen the Indian States and British Imperial government*, 1931.

Tarachand, *History of Freedom Novement in India*.

Tendulkar, *Mahatma, The Life of Mohandas Karamchand Gandhi*, Publication Divsion, Delhi, 1960-63.

Thompson, Edward, *Making of the Indian Prince*, Oxford University Press, London. 1943.

Thompson and Garrat, *Rise and fulfilment of British Rule in India*, Central Book Depot, Allahabad, 1958.

Vaijnath, *Riyasion Ka Sawal* (with a foreward by Pattabhi Sitaramayya) 1946.

Vardarajan, M.K., *The Indian States and the Federation*. Oxfard University Press, London, 1939.

Westlake, *Collected Papers*.

Index

E

F

G

H

I

J

K

L

M